Study

Presentation Skills for Students

www.skills4study.com – the leading study skills website

Palgrave Study Skills

Authoring a PhD
Business Degree Success
Career Skills
Critical Thinking Skills (2nd edn)
Cite them Right (8th edn)
e-Learning Skills (2nd edn)
Effective Communication for
  Arts and Humanities Students
Effective Communication for
  Science and Technology
The Exam Skills Handbook
The Foundations of Research (2nd edn)
The Good Supervisor
Great Ways to Learn Anatomy and
  Physiology
How to Manage your Arts, Humanities and
  Social Science Degree
How to Manage your Distance and
  Open Learning Course
How to Manage your Postgraduate Course
How to Manage your Science and
  Technology Degree
How to Study Foreign Languages
How to Study Linguistics (2nd edn)
How to Use your Reading in your Essays
How to Write Better Essays (2nd edn)
How to Write your Undergraduate
  Dissertation
Information Skills
IT Skills for Successful Study
Making Sense of Statistics
The International Student Handbook
The Mature Student's Guide to Writing (2nd edn)
The Mature Student's Handbook
The Palgrave Student Planner
The Personal Tutor's Handbook
The Postgraduate Research Handbook (2nd edn)

Presentation Skills for Students (2nd edn)
The Principles of Writing in Psychology
Professional Writing (2nd edn)
Researching Online
Research Using IT
Skills for Success (2nd edn)
The Study Abroad Handbook
The Student's Guide to Writing (2nd edn)
The Student Life Handbook
The Study Skills Handbook (3rd edn)
Study Skills for International Postgraduates
Study Skills for Speakers of English as
  a Second Language
Studying Arts and Humanities
Studying the Built Environment
Studying Business at MBA and Masters Level
Studying Economics
Studying History (3rd edn)
Studying Law (3rd edn)
Studying Mathematics and its Applications
Studying Modern Drama (2nd edn)
Studying Physics
Studying Programming
Studying Psychology (2nd edn)
Teaching Study Skills and Supporting Learning
The Undergraduate Research Handbook
The Work-Based Learning Student Handbook
Work Placements – A Survival Guide for Students
Writing for Law
Writing for Nursing and Midwifery Students (2nd edn)
Write it Right
Writing for Engineers (3rd edn)

Pocket Study Skills
Series Editor: Kate Williams

14 Days to Exam Success
Blogs, Wikis, Podcasts and More
Brilliant Writing Tips for Students
Completing Your PhD
Doing Research
Getting Critical
Planning Your Essay

Planning Your PhD
Reading and Making Notes
Referencing and Understanding Plagiarism
Science Study Skills
Success in Groupwork
Time Management
Writing for University

Presentation Skills for Students

2nd Edition

Joan van Emden and Lucinda Becker

palgrave
macmillan

First edition 2004
Second edition 2010
Published by
PALGRAVE MACMILLAN

Palgrave Macmillan in the UK is an imprint of Macmillan Publishers Limited, registered in England, company number 785998, of Houndmills, Basingstoke, Hampshire RG21 6XS.

Palgrave Macmillan in the US is a division of St Martin's Press LLC, 175 Fifth Avenue, New York, NY 10010.

Palgrave Macmillan is the global academic imprint of the above companies and has companies and representatives throughout the world.

Palgrave® and Macmillan® are registered trademarks in the United States, the United Kingdom, Europe and other countries.

ISBN-13: 978-0-230-24304-0

This book is printed on paper suitable for recycling and made from fully managed and sustained forest sources. Logging, pulping and manufacturing processes are expected to conform to the environmental regulations of the country of origin.

A catalogue record for this book is available from the British Library.

A catalog record for this book is available from the Library of Congress.

10 9 8 7 6 5 4 3
19 18 17 16 15 14 13 12 11

Printed in China

Contents

Preface

Presentation Skills for Students is a guide to the most transferable of all student skills and a critical part of professional development: the ability to present a case clearly, cogently and confidently. This is enormously valuable at every stage of students' lives, whatever subjects they study, helping them to achieve success in academic work, job interviews and their future working lives.

Presentation Skills was first published in 2004. The chapters which discuss body language, speaking as part of a group or controlling nerves are, of course, the same in 2010 and are unlikely to change, but in other respects, especially that of visual aids, technology has moved on, and this new edition reflects such developments.

We have included new material in the job search and job interviews chapter. We stress the use of the internet, and students are made aware of the potential hazards of social networking sites, such as Facebook, which may be used by employers to find out more about applicants before the interview stage. Extra illustrations, including cartoons, and new beginnings and endings to each chapter, make our book even more user-friendly.

This remains, to the best of our knowledge, the only book which gives practical help not only in making a wide range of presentations but also in topics such as standing at student elections and speaking as a student representative.

We have deliberately written in a friendly and readable style, with regular checklists and exercises to make it an invaluable book for students to dip into whenever they need help with speaking to an audience. All our advice comes from our long experience in making presentations and in teaching both students and professional people to speak with fluency and confidence.

We are grateful to everyone we have worked with for what they have taught us, and to colleagues and friends who have supported and encouraged us, especially John McGarvey for information about student union activities, and Anastasia and Felicity Becker for their careful and much-appreciated help with the index. As always, we are also grateful to our agent, Mandy Little, for her active help and encouragement.

JOAN VAN EMDEN AND LUCINDA BECKER
Reading, 2010

1 Personal Development: Speaking to an Audience

This chapter introduces you to:

▶ developing transfer-able skills and self-confidence
▶ choosing the right words
▶ assessing your ability to communicate in a range of situations
▶ the importance of listening

Developing your ability to speak to an audience is one of the greatest benefits you'll ever derive from your time in further or higher education. We've said 'developing', because it's likely that you've already had some experience of giving a talk, perhaps at school, for a club you belong to or in your place of work if you're a mature student. You will now have the chance to practise speaking effectively in a range of situations and in front of audiences of differing backgrounds and levels of knowledge. If you make the most of these opportunities, you will be gaining expertise which will be vital for your future and which may change you in ways you didn't expect when you began.

Let's look first at the practical outcome of your speaking abilities. A great deal is spoken and written nowadays about 'transferable skills' that you can carry into your future, whether you're going to stay in academic life, teach or follow any of the multitude of job opportunities that will present themselves. In years to come, you may well change not only jobs but also your career itself: it's possible to see an opportunity that you never dreamed of, and so to follow a new and exciting career path that you didn't know about when you first left education. Transferable skills are those that you can take with you: they're valuable for the rest of your life. The ability to speak well enough to interest, influence or persuade other people is a major asset, whatever you choose to do in the future.

You may also find that you gain in a more personal way. Many people are worried about talking to an audience and this is understandable – you may feel both nervous and vulnerable when you look for the first time at a roomful of people waiting to listen to you. This is a natural reaction and, as we'll discuss later, is in itself absolutely nothing to worry about. Most truly excellent speakers are nervous at the prospect of speaking. But – and this is the great advantage of having a go – once you've made a successful presentation, you will gain enormously in confidence. This in itself means that you are likely to make an even better presentation next time. Your new-found confidence may well affect other areas of your work, too: lecturers sometimes comment that after students have made their first presentation, they are more ready to ask questions, respond to a challenge and organise themselves and their work more effectively.

You will be preparing a personal development plan (PDP), probably in discussion with your tutor. This will give you the opportunity to think about yourself, how you learn, what motivates you, and so on. Part of this process is to help you to assess how your subject knowledge and career management skills are developing. Among the latter, you will be thinking about your transferable skills and how confident you are about using them. This book will help you with the specific skill of talking to an audience, not just as part of your coursework but also in your leisure time, whether you decide to become a student representative or just want to make a contribution at a society meeting. So what is involved in public speaking, and what influences us if we're in the audience?

When we talk to other people, whether formally or in conversation, we use at least three different techniques: we vary our voices, use changes of tone and reveal body language, a silent but eloquent way of sending a message. People's voices have qualities that may be attractive or unattractive: a low voice is usually easier to listen to than a high-pitched voice; a harsh voice can sound aggressive even when its owner feels at ease; a very soft voice may be pleasant at first, but becomes irritating if we, the listeners, have to concentrate hard to catch the words. Such qualities are not easy to change, but we're generally aware that we will speak more loudly if we're annoyed, more softly in an intimate setting, more rapidly if we're agitated and probably more slowly if we're not sure how to put across an idea.

Tone of voice is also very powerful in showing your meaning. Think of the many ways in which you can say something as simple as 'Thank you'. You can sound truly grateful, fully appreciative of the trouble someone has taken on your behalf, casual almost to the point of rudeness or impatient and sarcastic if you're not really feeling grateful at all. We use differences of tone to reflect an emotional response beyond the straightforward meaning of our words.

It's much harder to control our body language. This is conditioned largely by the cultural framework in which we grew up, but also by the situation in which we find ourselves at the time and the emotions we're feeling as we speak. It can reveal a state of mind which we'd prefer to keep quiet about, and in this way body language is both dangerous and important: it can give away responses we'd rather keep hidden, and it can either reinforce or contradict the words we use. Needless to say, we shall be looking at non-verbal communication (body language) in detail when we discuss making a presentation and attending an interview.

We've mentioned words, which are, of course, the principal medium for communicating our ideas to other people. Choosing the 'right' words is also a complex procedure, as it depends upon the meaning we want to convey, the person receiving the message and the situation in which the communication takes place. Out of the enormous range of words available in the English language, we have to choose those which most accurately reflect our meaning, and this is by no means an easy decision. Think of the words that can be used to convey the idea of a pleasant feeling of general goodwill: cheerfulness, jollity, merriment, pleasure, joy, happiness. We can see at once that these words have similar meanings but they aren't interchangeable: merriment might last only for a moment or two at the end of a joke, while joy suggests a much deeper and more lasting emotion. If we want to influence an audience, we have to choose our words carefully so that they reflect our meaning as closely as possible.

Our choice of words is also conditioned both by the person who is going to hear them and the situation in which we find ourselves. If we're talking to a friend, we can usually be informal or even careless about our words, knowing that the recipient will understand our meaning even if we don't express ourselves very clearly; if we are speaking to a prospective employer, we will be much more formal and careful about the words we choose. If our friend is part of a large audience to which we're giving a formal presentation, the situation will override the individual and our approach will be formal in spite of the presence of the friend.

If speaking is clearly an art we need to think about carefully, so too is listening. We depend on the goodwill of the people who hear our words: do they really want to listen? Do they know how to interpret our tone of voice and our body language? Are they preoccupied with their own thoughts? Is their knowledge of the language we're speaking good enough for our purposes? We'll be looking at some aspects of the listening process in more detail later and also suggesting ways in which we can help our listeners to concentrate on our message.

In your course, you'll be expected to listen well and speak effectively. This will be in one-to-one situations, for example at meetings with your tutor, in small groups such as seminars and as you make formal presentations, perhaps as part of a team. Many of these occasions will be assessed, some as part of your final exam result. In your leisure time, you will want to make the most of opportunities to join clubs and societies, and take a leading role when the time is right. You may want to stand for election to office and, if you're elected, may then have to introduce outside speakers and chair meetings. You may represent your student group on an important and influential body such as your hall of residence management committee or university senate.

All these responsibilities depend to a large extent on your ability to speak clearly, concisely and convincingly. If you can do this, not only will you be making the most of your academic and social life, but you will also have developed both personal confidence and a useful, transferable skill to take into your future career.

Top Tips
- Think positively
- Develop your transferable skills and your own confidence
- Read the rest of this book!

2 Delivery, Non-verbal Communication and Nerves

This chapter helps you to:

▶ set up good speaking habits
▶ control the volume and speed of your speech
▶ practise speaking clearly and with appropriate emphasis
▶ use silence effectively
▶ recognise how we use body language
▶ use non-verbal communication (NVC) to emphasise your message
▶ make eye contact with your audience
▶ control your nerves and use them to your advantage

In some ways, this is the most important chapter in the book. In it, we want to look in detail at speaking situations and the major tools you'll be using as you speak: your voice and your body language.

We mentioned these topics in Chapter 1, and stressed how many considerations you have to keep in mind in order to be a good speaker. It isn't easy, but, as with most aspects of spoken communication, you'll find that you improve rapidly with practice. From our point of view as lecturers, it's one of the most rewarding parts of teaching such skills: provided that students really want to improve, they will; each presentation is likely to be better than the previous one.

This is partly because what we try to do is to set up good speaking habits. Most poor presenting is the result of bad habits such as not looking at the audience or muttering instead of speaking clearly. Yet most people are quite capable of making eye contact and speaking clearly; they may not even realise that they don't do these things, and it can come as quite a shock if they see a video of their performance. If they then take one aspect of their presentation, such as their poor enunciation, and work at improving it, they will find that not only will their words soon become clearer but they will also start to speak more clearly as a matter of habit, without having to think about it at all. They can then take the next feature they want to improve and work at setting up another good habit. In this way, they will, surprisingly quickly, become better presenters as well as gaining more confidence – and confidence, as we shall see, is one of the keys to speaking well.

In most chapters in this book, we've given you regular checklists to help you to put our advice into practice. In this chapter, there's just one near the beginning, which helps you to assess the qualities of your own voice, perhaps with the help of a friend. After that, we've suggested exercises which will help you to become aware of your voice and your NVC and show you how to use them effectively.

● Using your voice

Voice checklist

It's a good idea to start this section by thinking about your own voice. Ask yourself some questions:

- ❑ Is my voice loud, perhaps too loud?
- ❑ Is my voice soft, perhaps too soft?
- ❑ Do I speak too slowly?
- ❑ Do I speak too quickly?
- ❑ Is my voice monotonous?
- ❑ Do I articulate clearly or do I mutter?
- ❑ Will my accent cause my audience any particular difficulty?
- ❑ Do I run out of breath and gasp for air as I speak?

You may be unsure about the answers to some of these questions, but, if so, we expect that your friends will help you out!

Volume

Let's start with the first and second questions, which obviously belong together. Is your voice too loud or too soft? You may be interested to know that a 'yes' answer to the first question is comparatively rare. While loud voices aren't uncommon, voices which are too loud for the setting and circumstances in which they're used are unusual, and the owner of such a voice is likely to be aware of the problem.

Loud voices If you have a naturally loud voice, you obviously have a built-in advantage: people are going to be able to hear you. You will probably find it easy to assert yourself, which means that you must take care not to trample on other people's ideas if they're different from yours. If you're working as part of a group, always try to listen to other points of view before giving your own, and see if it's possible for you to start by saying something friendly, such as 'I really like what you're suggesting, but perhaps . . .', rather than going straight for the disagreement.

When you talk to an audience, either a small group or a large number, you will be helped, as most people are, by trying out the room or lecture theatre in advance. Take a friend with you and ask him or her to sit at the back. First of all, speak naturally and check whether you can be heard. Then try decreasing the volume slightly, as long as your friend can hear easily from the back of the room. Remember that people absorb sound, so when the room is full, you'll need a little more volume than when it's empty. However, there's only a small difference and you mustn't exaggerate. Speak several times at what you and your friend feel is the right volume. You may find that nerves make you want to speak more loudly, but now that you've established the right volume for the space, try to reproduce that same feeling. It may take a bit of practice, but you're setting up the good habit of adjusting the volume at which you speak to suit the venue.

Sometimes, of course, you'll be speaking in a small space such as your tutor's room and will need to adjust to the different environment. Speak more slowly and with more pauses (see also pp. 11, 18–21), and watch for the reactions of the people you're speaking to – if they tend to move away or sit right back in the seat, you may be overwhelming them with sound. If you can lower the pitch of your voice (see pp. 9–10), this will help; it's essential that you don't raise the pitch and shout, which is hard on your voice and uncomfortable for the listener.

Later in this section, we'll be suggesting some voice exercises for people who speak too softly. You might also like to try them, especially those connected with breathing correctly. You could, for instance, use the humming exercise (p. 10) and concentrate on gradually reducing the sound rather than increasing it.

Soft voices   You are much more likely to discover that your voice is too soft and that people can't easily hear you. Is this always the case or is it only when it's a formal occasion and you're speaking to an audience? If you decide that it's the latter, then ask yourself why this is so. Do you hate speaking in public so much that you instinctively want to hide from people, to withdraw into your own space where you have to speak only to yourself?

If you feel like this, you need to build up confidence – but don't try too much all at once. Here are some ways in which you can help yourself: don't

Don't try to hide from the audience!

expect instant results, but with every achievement, you'll increase your chances of success next time:

- Join in small group conversations, even if it's only to say a few words.
- Agree with another speaker out loud. Don't just think, 'What a good idea' – say so. You'll please someone else in the group as well as gaining confidence by hearing your own voice.
- Try to ask a question in a seminar group. Work out in advance what you want to say and, if possible, tell a friend in the group, so that he or she can support you and perhaps agree with you as soon as you've finished.
- Be willing to take a tutor or lecturer into your confidence. If you can see that you're going to have to speak by yourself, either to read a seminar paper or make a presentation on your project, tell the member of staff in charge how difficult this is for you. He or she may well let you sit down rather than stand, or let you share a paper so that someone else will do some of the talking. Give him or her the chance to be supportive.
- If you can, play a very small role in a group activity. If you have to say just a couple of sentences, your ordeal will be short, and if your

group is supporting you, you will be helped to feel really pleased with yourself afterwards.

- Always go in advance to the room in which you have to speak, and sit or stand in the position you'll need to take. Look round at the empty space and make yourself at ease with it as far as possible, so that it seems familiar when the time comes.
- Read all that we say about nerves (pp. 30–3) and try out our advice.
- Always praise yourself for any achievement, however small, and encourage your friends to congratulate you, too. The better you feel, the more confident you will be and the more you will be able to project your voice.

When you find yourself rehearsing before you speak to a real audience, imagine a friend sitting at the back of the room. Ignore the other people who'll be there and focus on giving your information to just this one friend. You'll need to throw your voice out so that your friend can hear you and also keep your head up so that you can see him or her. Rehearse this and you'll be setting up a good habit for the event itself.

Voice Exercise 1

Go into an empty room and stand at one end. Now think of some words which have explosive sounds, such as 'Stop!', 'Crash!' and 'Bang!' Imagine a scene in which you need to shout one of these words (someone is about to walk under a bus, and you yell 'Stop!'), then do so, very loudly, and notice as you do how you take a deep breath and move your mouth quite instinctively. Now try saying the words again, this time not shouting, but speaking as loudly as you can, taking a breath and moving your mouth as before. When you've tried this a few times, use other words which don't have quite such a forceful sound – perhaps 'Good morning', as the hard 'g' sound has something of the same impact.

This will help you if you don't move your lips enough – a common reason for people speaking too softly. You might also like to try the articulation exercise on p. 15.

Perhaps you're not suffering unduly from nerves but just have a naturally soft voice. The advice in the following paragraph will help you too, but you may need to practise some voice exercises in order to increase your volume. There's one above and one over the page.

Breath control Your breathing supports your voice, which is why we've included this exercise under 'Volume'; if you breathe well, you can increase the volume of sound that you produce just by pressing gently on the diaphragm, as

Voice Exercise 2

Part of your problem when making too little noise might be that you are swallowing your words, keeping your voice far too much at the back of your throat. If you hum, you'll see that the sound comes much more from the mask of your face than from so far back. Humming also helps with breathing properly, essential if you're to speak well. Do you breathe shallowly, so that you just expand your chest space and raise your shoulders? Try to take a deep breath so that you expand your diaphragm – you should feel the movement right down at the belt of your jeans. Put your hands on your ribcage and feel how it expands, but don't let your shoulders move upwards. Think of taking a breath as filling a jug: start as low as you can, right down at the diaphragm, and gradually fill the space in your body until you have an enormous reserve of air to support your voice.

When you've taken a good, deep breath, hum on one note for as long as you can, letting out your breath in a slow, controlled way. You should be able to keep the note going for at least 20 seconds and probably more. If you're a good athlete, or you sing or play a wind instrument, you will probably manage at least 40 seconds. Do this exercise each day, and you will be able gradually to extend the length of your humming note. Sometimes, start humming very quietly and slowly increase the sound by putting a slight pressure on your diaphragm and then decrease it again. You're learning to control your breathing, which is very important for public speaking. At the same time, you're discovering a way of reducing stress, as deep, controlled breathing relaxes you both physically and mentally. We'll say more about this when we discuss nerves and how to use them.

you will do when you are humming in Exercise 2 – much better than trying to force your vocal cords, which are delicate and easily injured.

When you talk to an audience, you'll find that all your breathing work has had a good effect – you will be breathing well as a matter of habit, and you'll find that you can gradually increase the volume with which you speak. It won't happen all at once, of course, and your voice may continue to be soft, but your audience will have a better chance of hearing everything that you say. Look at them as you speak, especially the people in the back row, and remember that you have to throw your voice out for them to hear, just as you did when you shouted 'Stop!' in an empty room.

Pace
Slow speech Now it's time we looked at the second pair of questions about your voice: do you speak too slowly or do you speak too quickly? It's very unlikely that you speak too slowly, although sometimes people achieve this effect by breaking up the words they want to say so that there seem to be

pauses in places where they aren't helpful to the listeners. Do you think that you might talk (in public) in the way illustrated below?

> *Good morning . . . everyone . . . Today we'd like . . . to present . . .*
> *to you . . . what seem to us . . . to be the major causes . . .*
> *of the general strike . . . in 1926. We'll speak for . . . about . . .*
> *20 minutes . . . and then . . . we'll be happy to answer . . .*
> *any questions you may have.*

If you do speak like this, it's very likely that you have the right attitude, in that you know that it's important to talk slowly to an audience and that a good speaker uses pauses in order to break up the content of the talk into manageable chunks of information. But a message can be broken up too much, so that the listener has no sense of a group of words making a sensible pattern; pauses occur so often and in such unexpected places that they lose their significance. The overall effect is that the speaker is talking slowly, but the individual words themselves may be rushed: the pauses give the impression that very little is said in the time available.

If we look again at the passage above, we'll see that the words fall into groups which produce meaning: 'Good morning, everybody', is such a group; the next is 'Today we'd like to present to you'. It's probably better to leave out 'what seem to us to be', as it sounds unnecessarily hesitant – if you didn't think that these were the major causes, why would you be presenting them? If you were giving them as someone else's point of view, you would say so straightaway: 'Joe Bloggs's view of the major causes . . .' The next group of words, which are the most important, introduces your subject: 'the major causes of the general strike in 1926'. Within this phrase, you will stress the key elements: major, general strike, 1926 and, although slightly less so, causes. It isn't a long phrase, however, and you should be able to say it easily and clearly in one breath. Don't be tempted to rush the words, as it's essential that the audience knows what your subject is, but don't break them up.

Your next group of words consists of: 'We'll speak for about twenty minutes', which has a unity of meaning, after which you can finish with the last group, 'and then we'll be happy to answer any questions you may have'. If you find it difficult to manage all this in one breath, then look back at the voice exercises on pages 9 and 10 and practise your breathing.

Whatever your pace of speaking, it's important that you don't break up the flow of meaning. The audience has only the one chance to hear what you want to say, and, as listening isn't particularly easy, you need to phrase everything you say so that it can be followed and understood as readily as possible. If you do this, you will also be able to use pauses to good effect, as we'll show in the later section 'Using silence'.

Fast speech It's far more likely, however, that your problem is one of excessive speed. Many speakers, particularly those who are inexperienced and very nervous, speak too quickly. You might make a note for yourself on your script or on your cards to remind you at regular intervals to slow down. Let's now look in more detail at the question of fast speaking.

One cause is undoubtedly the speaker's state of mind. If you approach your presentation by thinking that you're going to find it a terrible ordeal and you just wish it were over, then inevitably your subconscious will suggest that if you speak quickly, it will soon all be over, and indeed that's true. The effect you have on the audience, however, will be much less satisfactory, and it's worth considering the whole event from their point of view.

Members of the audience have come to hear you because either they have to (it's part of their course) or they want to hear what you have to say. Both may of course be the case. What they don't want is to feel that they've wasted their time, and so, by and large, they're ready to listen.

Listening is difficult. Your audience is likely to start with considerable goodwill towards you (not least because they're grateful that it's you speaking and not them), and they listen at first in the hope of finding that you've chosen an interesting subject about which they may learn something. If they can easily hear what you say, they will tend to go on listening, and if you are obviously interested in what you're saying, they will pick up on your interest and so be willing to carry on listening (which is why, later, we'll stress the importance of your enthusiasm). If you speak slowly, they will have time not only to hear what you say, but also to understand and assimilate it, make it part of their own knowledge base and, perhaps, think of a useful question to ask. If you speak quickly, there simply isn't time for this process to take place; even if they manage the first part, hearing, or even the second part, understanding, they won't have time to assimilate the information and make it theirs. As a result, they will remember very little and will feel that they have gained no long-term benefit from being present.

Think well of your audience. See them as friends, and as people who want to learn from you because they're interested in what you have to say. It's the truth anyway, and it will help you to speak slowly for their benefit.

A common problem is speaking from a full script and so being tempted to read rather than to speak. Whether you use a full text or notes, you need to mark them up so that you know when to pause, lift your head and look at the audience. You also need to be as familiar as possible with what you want to say, so that you don't lose your place just because you're pausing and looking at the audience. There is also a marked difference in speed between reading, talking informally and speaking to an audience: you need to practise speaking slowly so that this becomes a good habit which you can use whenever you need to. If you're going to speak at the recommended speed of about 100–110 words a minute, you'll need to try this out and see what it feels like. It will seem odd at first, but persevere and it will soon become acceptable.

Voice Exercise 3

By a lucky coincidence, the paragraph above, beginning 'Listening is difficult', contains 198 words, which is ideal for the purpose of practice. Read the paragraph aloud and time yourself, and try again until you manage to take about a minute and a half to read it. Depending on the size of the audience, that's just about the speed you need when you talk in public.

Rushed activity Sometimes, speed is a question of movement as a whole rather than just of speech. If you rush your entry, start to speak too quickly, snatch at visual aids and dash between projector and screen, you are setting up an atmosphere of speed which is likely to be reflected in your words. One of the most useful things you can do is to get the right rhythm at the beginning of your talk. If you have to walk forward to the dais or the front of the room, walk briskly but don't appear to be on the verge of running. Now stand and look at the audience, and when they look as if they're ready, greet them. Pause and smile round at them for a moment before you speak again. You will benefit in two ways: you will have looked friendly and welcoming to those who have come to hear you, and you will have allowed yourself time to take control of the situation. You are then much less likely to rush either your activity or your words.

Speaking clearly

If you have your volume and pace under control, you already have huge assets in talking to an audience, but you still need to ensure that you're articulating all the important parts of words, and not swallowing the sound.

Dropping your voice The rhythms of the English language aren't helpful. We tend to drop our voices as we approach the end of our sentences, which can have the effect of 'hiding' the last word or two, leaving the audience to guess what we said. If, at the same moment, we turn to look at the screen or look down at our notes, those last few words may be completely inaudible. In the same way, an aside can be irritatingly difficult to hear: everything we say in front of an audience should be clearly heard by them. If we make a little comment for our own benefit, such as a muttered 'At least, I hope that's the right date', or 'Well, I think so', the audience is left not knowing whether they should have heard what we said (but didn't quite catch it) or whether we weren't talking to them (but why not, in a presentation?).

Local accents Think about your own accent. Most native English speakers have a regional accent of some kind, even if it's very slight, and if English isn't your first language, you may have a strong accent which, in terms of your student group, is particular to you. This is clearly a good thing, as it would be just as boring if we all sounded the same as it would be if we all looked the same. Nevertheless, you must be certain that if you're talking to an audience, they can understand every word you say. If your accent makes you swallow particular sounds, you may find that some words are unclear. For example, a London/south-east accent tends to lose 't' sounds, so that a speaker might say compu'er rather than computer, or in'ermi'ent for intermittent. Now the first example, compu'er, would probably be clear enough to the audience, but by the time two letters in a word are swallowed, in'ermi'ent, the word is being distorted to the point at which it isn't easy to follow. As you think about your own voice, try to decide whether there are some words which you have difficulty in saying clearly – again, a friend might be able to help you.

If your subject of study is scientific or technical, it's especially important that you sound all your words clearly. Inevitably, you will be using a specialist vocabulary containing complex terms, and the audience must be able either to recognise them or to remember them later in order to ask a question or check in a subject dictionary. Voice Exercise 4, below, gives you some difficult expressions to try out; make sure that you can pronounce them clearly, articulating every syllable so that the audience has no doubt about what you said.

Using your mouth When you speak, do you move your mouth almost as if you were chewing toffee? One of the most common reasons for poor articulation, not sounding every part of a word clearly, is that the mouth isn't used fully. Notice how some speakers hardly move their lips as they speak and how hard it is to hear their words. If you're projecting your voice to a large audience, make sure that you exaggerate the movements of your mouth – it will feel odd at first, and you may feel that you sound unnatural, but you are helping your listeners to catch every sound and follow every word. Here are some expressions for you to practise saying.

Voice Exercise 4

First of all, imagine that you have a large piece of sticky toffee in your mouth and you're trying not to let it stick to your teeth. Fortunately, there isn't anybody else around, so you can chew as violently as you like. Do this for a moment or two, as it's a good exercise to loosen up the muscles of your jaw and mouth before you begin to speak.

Now say the following phrases aloud, making sure that you make every sound as precisely and energetically as you can:

Electromagnetic compatibility
(Was every 't' sound clear?)

A medieval knight wearing helmet, hauberk and armour-cap
(Are the repeated 't' and 'h' sounds clear? Did you say 'darmour'?)

Romantics, realists and impressionists
(Did you avoid the trap of 'dimpressionists'?)

Peas, beans, broccoli and cauliflowers
(Are you really making your mouth work hard?)

Hemidemisemiquaver
(Yes, this really exists, but can you say it clearly?)

As you practise speaking in public, imagine that among your audience there are a few people who have a hearing disability (it could happen). They need to supplement their listening by watching your mouth, by lip-reading. Interestingly, most of us lip-read to a certain extent if we get the chance, although we're generally not aware of doing so. Now you have to use your mouth so that you give as much help as possible to your listeners: if you don't move your mouth or open your lips very far, some of them won't know what you're saying. This exercise has another advantage: it will make you aware of the need to face your audience all the time you're talking. If you turn to face the screen or put your head down as you speak, some people won't be able to take in what you said. If, at the end of your practice, a friend at the back of the room feels that your imaginary audience will have had the best chance you can possibly give them to hear, understand and assimilate your words, you're speaking clearly.

Variation in speech rhythms

It's a common problem: a speaker has interesting material, but a voice which drones on and on at the same speed and volume until the audience feels positively drowsy. If you've worked through the exercises so far, you'll certainly be heard, but if you're going to capture your audience, you must vary the rhythms of your speech.

Some people are lucky enough to be born with voices that are flexible and lively; others just sound monotonous, no matter how excited they are by their subject. You now have to make sure that your voice sounds interesting, not just to make it easier to listen to but also to tell your audience how they have to approach what you want to say. First, it's useful to think how you speak in everyday conversation. If you approach a group of friends in order to tell them some exciting good news, you instinctively raise your voice to attract attention and then speak in a way that reflects your excitement, with emphasis and stress on key words, and eloquent pauses ('What do you think happened then?', with a pause for them to guess). Suppose instead that you have to give them directions for getting to your house. You speak much more slowly, pause, watch them to see if they appear to understand and repeat the key details to help them ('It's the third turning on the right, don't forget, the third'). Now imagine that you want to ask the group an important question. You may wait for a moment or two and make sure that you really have their attention ('Hang on a moment, I want to ask if any of you . . .'). You'll then wait to hear their reply, and the more difficult the question, the longer you'll be willing to wait.

Giving emphasis The same kind of variety is essential when you're talking to an audience. You want to attract their attention to what you feel is an exciting subject, so you must look and sound excited. Allow your face to light up and your tone of voice to be bright and positive. Make sure that you start slowly and with emphasis, and tell them how interesting the topic is. Help them to feel that they want to listen to you. Stress the key words – remember the example of the general strike that we used earlier and how you had to make sure that people listening knew exactly what you were going to talk about.

If you have more complex information to give, perhaps technical or scientific detail, it's much more like the road directions. Slow down, pause, repeat the key details, say the same thing but in a different way, and, above all, don't overwhelm your audience by trying to say too much too fast. From time to time, ask the audience a question, but make sure that, when you've given them time to think, you supply the answer yourself. They mustn't feel threatened because it seems as if in some way you're giving them a kind of test.

You may want to tell the audience what their approach should be. Not everything you say will be of equal importance: some details will be trivial, but perhaps included as a touch of light relief or a personal comment. The audience has to know what matters, and the way in which you use your voice will tell them. If you want them to take in something of major importance, you need to slow down, pause for a moment and speak slightly more loudly and emphatically than before. The tone of your voice will then make it clear that this is an important statement. Once you've told them this key fact, pause to let them take it in. Then speed up very slightly and lower the volume just a trace (but make sure that they can still hear clearly) and they will realise that you have moved on to a lesser point.

If you feel that it'll be difficult to remember this emphasis when you're speaking, mark up your script or notes, perhaps using a highlighter pen on the points you want to stress. It's also helpful to recognise that we give emphasis naturally to the first part of a sentence; what follows has a reduced stress and so appears to be less important.

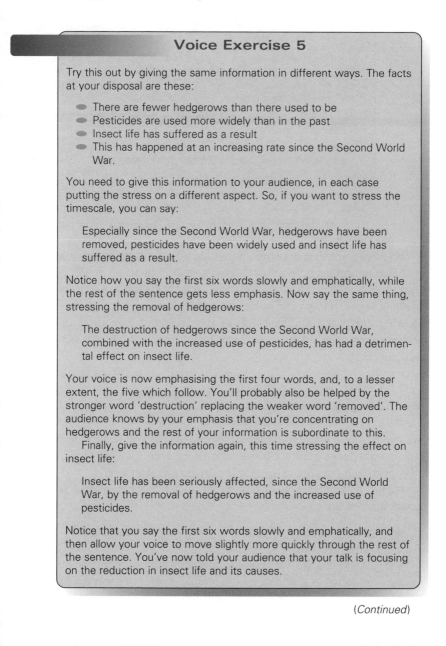

Voice Exercise 5

Try this out by giving the same information in different ways. The facts at your disposal are these:

- There are fewer hedgerows than there used to be
- Pesticides are used more widely than in the past
- Insect life has suffered as a result
- This has happened at an increasing rate since the Second World War.

You need to give this information to your audience, in each case putting the stress on a different aspect. So, if you want to stress the timescale, you can say:

> Especially since the Second World War, hedgerows have been removed, pesticides have been widely used and insect life has suffered as a result.

Notice how you say the first six words slowly and emphatically, while the rest of the sentence gets less emphasis. Now say the same thing, stressing the removal of hedgerows:

> The destruction of hedgerows since the Second World War, combined with the increased use of pesticides, has had a detrimental effect on insect life.

Your voice is now emphasising the first four words, and, to a lesser extent, the five which follow. You'll probably also be helped by the stronger word 'destruction' replacing the weaker word 'removed'. The audience knows by your emphasis that you're concentrating on hedgerows and the rest of your information is subordinate to this.

Finally, give the information again, this time stressing the effect on insect life:

> Insect life has been seriously affected, since the Second World War, by the removal of hedgerows and the increased use of pesticides.

Notice that you say the first six words slowly and emphatically, and then allow your voice to move slightly more quickly through the rest of the sentence. You've now told your audience that your talk is focusing on the reduction in insect life and its causes.

(Continued)

Voice Exercise 5 (Continued)

In each case, you've given the audience additional information, beyond the meaning of the words. You need to do this, so that your listeners know what's important and what you think about the subject. Try a rather different example:

Many fine old trees have been cut down to make way for much-needed halls of residence.

Make it clear, as you say this, that in spite of the need for halls of residence, you really regret the loss of the trees. Notice how you say the words 'fine' and 'old' slowly and emphatically, probably lengthening the 'o' sound in the word 'old'. You've conveyed your personal feelings without actually spelling them out. Now change your opinion: you are sorry about the trees, but the need for halls of residence is paramount:

Some much-needed halls of residence have been built, although sadly some fine old trees have had to be cut down.

Make sure that you give a lot of stress to 'much-needed' and say the last part of the sentence rather more quickly, and even the word 'sadly' doesn't change the fact that you approve of the new building!

You'll have seen that in using your voice for emphasis in this way, you've met two important criteria for talking successfully to an audience: you've told them how they should understand your message, without awkwardly spelling it out, and you've achieved variety in your voice by speeding up, slowing down and emphasising the key words. If you use your voice in this way, you are going to be easy to listen to, which will delight your audience.

● Using silence

A large part of a successful presentation takes place in silence. In fact, it's a sign of experience and confidence when a speaker is willing to allow silence to happen without feeling the need to fill the gap with words.

There are moments in talking to an audience when silence is natural. Some of these are:

- at the beginning of your talk, when you're waiting for the audience to settle down
- as you change a visual aid, whether it's moving acetate on to the projector or just clicking the remote control to show a new image

- when you finish one aspect of your subject, and pause before moving on to the next
- in a natural way, when you give emphasis to a particular aspect
- if you're part of a group of speakers, when one person finishes and the audience waits for the next speaker
- when you finish your talk and ask for questions.

It's worth looking at each of these occasions in more detail.

Silence at the start

The beginning of a talk is difficult and it's important not to rush into speech. Look at your audience and assess when they're ready to listen. Smile at them before you greet them. It's unlikely that you'll have to wait more than a few seconds, although if you're very nervous, it might feel like ten minutes. They need that time to help them to settle down and focus their attention, and so do you. The silence helps you to feel in control of the situation and to develop the habit of not rushing (see pp. 12–13).

Pauses in your talk

In Chapter 3, we'll say much more about the timing of visual aids, but we need to stress now that, whatever type of aid you're using, showing it will add to the length of your presentation. You need to make sure that it's correctly displayed on the screen, and the audience needs to look at it and understand it. If you start to speak too quickly, they aren't ready and will miss something of what you say.

The pause between sections of your talk is also helpful to both you and the people who are listening. As you complete the beginning of your talk, for example, and move on to the more complex information, pause for a moment to let the audience register the change. You then have that moment to take a breath and prepare yourself for the next stage. Again, we talk about this in more detail in looking at the structure of a presentation (see p. 96). In many ways, a group presentation has its own clear pauses, for example as each speaker finishes and goes to sit down. If the next speaker starts to speak too soon, for instance as he or she walks forward, there's too much activity going on and the audience won't be concentrating fully.

The pause before questions is particularly important, as it gives the audience time to think, judge whether a question is appropriate and find the right words. You mustn't rush this process.

These are the major, natural pauses, but there are others, one of the most useful being the pause that alerts the audience to the importance of what follows. We've already discussed ways of avoiding monotony and giving emphasis, and silence is another useful technique. As you approach a key message in your talk, pause briefly before you introduce it: the silence lets the audience know that they must listen carefully to what follows. As you finish your key statement, pause in the same way again before moving on, so that they know you've completed what you wanted to stress.

Numbers

Pauses are essential in the case of numbers, which are always difficult to hear accurately. If, for instance, you wanted to say, 'A massive meteor impact about sixty-five million years ago resulted in an impact crater a hundred and thirteen miles wide in the Yucatan Peninsula', you would have included two figures that the audience needed to absorb. The first isn't too bad as it's not exact anyway, but there is one small difficulty, which is that the last letter of the preceding word, 't', joins easily to the first sound of the figure, 's'. We tend to say 'about sixty' as if it were all one word. Make sure that you separate the words 'about' and 'sixty', even if it feels artificial to do so. Look again at the section above about speaking clearly, where we discuss in more detail the need to separate sounds.

The other figure, 'a hundred and thirteen', is much more difficult to say clearly. The difference in sound between 'thirteen' and 'thirty' is very slight, and when it's preceded by 'a hundred', we're distracted and don't listen as carefully as we should. The problem would be even greater if the following word began with 'n', as in 'just thirteen notes'.

The most helpful way to clarify the numbers is to give a tiny pause just before and just after the number itself: say, 'a crater/a hundred and thirteen/miles wide', or, in the second example, 'just/thirteen/notes'. The slight pause represented by the oblique stroke allows the listener to separate the sounds and so identify what each represents. If the number is particularly important, spell it out numerically (one/one/three) or include it in a visual aid on the screen.

Problem pauses

These are all pauses that the speaker chooses to employ, but there's also one more which happens for a different reason: you've forgotten what you're going to say next. Don't worry – it happens to all speakers occasionally, and if you have good notes, it won't be a serious problem. Give yourself time to think and look at your notes in silence. It will in fact be a very short pause, even though it seems ages to you, the speaker. Don't try to fill this gap: if you just pause as you have done for other reasons, the audience, if it notices at all, will simply assume that it's a pause for effect. However, if you try to fill the silence by saying 'er' or 'um', then of course they know that you've got a problem. The golden rule is not to let the audience know about any difficulties unless you have to – and in this case, you don't.

All these pauses, short in themselves, add up to a surprising amount of silence. The audience will be happy about this, as it gives them time for the essential process we mentioned earlier: listening, understanding, assimilating. It also helps you, as you say less in the time available, stay in control and give yourself useful thinking time. You will be much less likely to run out of breath and gasp for air, as you're giving yourself breathing time, too. Above all, you sound authoritative because you have the confidence to allow silence to happen.

● Listening to voices

Human voices are fascinating, both in themselves and in the ways in which they are used. Watch and listen to a range of speakers, and notice how they make use of their voices, asking yourself the following questions:

- Quality of voice: is it soft, harsh, musical, flat?
- Volume and pace: can you hear easily, and have you the time to listen, understand and assimilate the information?
- Use of voice: does the speaker vary the volume and pace, emphasising the key issues?
- Articulation: can you hear and identify each word, including difficult and unfamiliar terms?
- Silence: does the speaker pause regularly, and how do you use these silences?

As you become more aware of the effect other people's voices have on you, think about the effect of your own voice on those who hear you. If you use it well, you will notice that people really listen and respond to what you say. How can you build an even stronger relationship with an audience? Your voice needs to be supported by effective NVC, and that's what we'll now discuss.

● Using NVC

Cultural setting
Before we look at body language in detail, we must make it clear that we're assuming that you will be speaking within the UK, or at least Western Europe. NVC is strongly linked to culture, and it wouldn't be wise to take the

advice we give in this section and use it indiscriminately in front of, for example, a Japanese audience. If you find yourself preparing to speak to an audience in a different part of the world from your own, check with your contacts whether there's any specific aspect of body language which you should avoid, or whether there's something that the audience would expect from you.

Having said this, we should add that you can't easily change your body language in a radical way. We'll be giving you lots of advice about using it effectively, but it's unlikely that, in everyday life, you can make it very different – and you'd be causing problems for yourself if you tried. If you speak a foreign language well, you will realise that you do modify your body language as you speak the other language, but it takes a high level of fluency to do this both automatically and convincingly.

You may, of course, be a student who has English as your second or even third language. If so, you will realise that some of your body language is different from that of other students, and sometimes you may fail to interpret their meaning accurately. Nevertheless, as you're using English for study, you will be reasonably at ease with it, and so the differences of NVC aren't likely to cause you much difficulty. Certainly, it isn't sensible to give yourself extra anxiety by trying to conform exactly to what other students do naturally, and in any case the audience will be sympathetic and impressed that you're doing so well in a language that isn't your own.

Everyday body language

In ordinary life, we use body language all the time, mostly without thinking about it, and we recognise it in other people. Practise identifying different aspects of NVC in everyday situations (see the exercise below). How does this apply to a seminar or presentation? The most important relationship on these occasions is that between you, the speaker, and the audience, and all of you will be using body language. You will be using it to build the essential rapport which convinces your listeners of what you're saying and encourages their response; they will be using it to reflect how they feel about your presenting skills (impressed, encouraged, bored) and about your message (interested, agreeing, disagreeing). It's essential, therefore, that you use appropriate NVC as you speak and that you recognise the signals that the audience is sending out.

So let's go through a presentation, looking at the appropriate body language at each stage. If you're using a full script or a lectern, you will be more restricted, but you will still be using body language as far as you can.

Body Language Exercise 1

As you sit in a lecture, take a moment or two to look round. If it's a good lecture, notice how other students are leaning forward, watching the lecturer and obviously concentrating. If it's a boring lecture (and some are!), notice that some students may be leaning back in their seats, perhaps looking out of the window, moving restlessly and obviously not concentrating.

If you are out in the evening, perhaps in a local pub, watch other people's actions, especially if you can't hear their words. If two people are deep in conversation, try to assess whether they're happy with the situation, whether one of them perhaps wants to get away or whether they're arguing. Look around for someone who's bored, waiting anxiously for a friend to arrive or very tired. How do you know? You can't hear them, you don't know them, but they're sending out all these messages by their body language, and you are picking up the messages and interpreting them.

NVC at the start of your talk

The first action that an audience takes when you appear on the scene is to look at you. You may be sitting at the top of the table and they come to join you; you may already be in the audience and have to come to the front; you may walk into the room and take your place when they are already there. However you appear in front of your audience, they will look at you and start to make up their minds about you long before you speak. What do they see?

If you put your head down, fail to look at the people in front of you, hunch your shoulders and shuffle your feet, they may reasonably assume that you don't want to talk to them. You're there under protest and you're going to take your irritation out on them. Their immediate reaction is likely to be that if you don't want to talk to them, they don't want to listen to you. You've started to make a poor relationship with them without saying a word.

On the other hand, you might rush into the room (up to the table or whatever), give them a quick glance and half a smile, sit down as quickly as possible and keep your head down. You're clearly nervous, but you know that you need to show some awareness of the audience and its reactions. The audience will be sympathetic about your nerves (see pp. 30–3) and perhaps sorry for you, but also apprehensive. If you're so uptight before you even start to speak, will you actually manage to talk to them? Suppose that you can't, and you break down and they are embarrassed. You've established a wary relationship with them: they're unsure about what's to follow and they're reserving their judgement to see what happens.

I'm scared   I'm confident

Let's try a different scene. You walk in at a brisk but unhurried pace, your head is up and your first action is to look round and smile at the audience. As you reach your place, you either sit or stand in an alert posture, looking as if you really want to talk to the people in front of you. What happens? As you smile at the audience, they will smile back (people do), which makes them feel good because smiling is a pleasant action, and it encourages you because you can see that their first response is friendly. They're impressed by your obvious confidence and so, reasonably, they assume that you have something interesting to say and that you want to say it. They settle down happily to wait for you to start.

You haven't said a word yet, but you've already built up a relationship with your audience, and once it's established in this way, it's surprisingly difficult to change it. It's therefore important that it should be a good relationship, one which will support you throughout your talk, and so we'll analyse the details of body language that we gave in the previous paragraph.

Walking
The way you walk is a clue to your emotions. Think of this in ordinary life: if you feel cheerful, you have a lively, almost bouncy style of walking; if you feel miserable, you tend to look down and move more slowly and heavily. You need to convey a cheerful message to your audience in the way you walk.

There's an essential comment that we must make at this stage: if your walk and the other aspects of your NVC are the result of your emotions, you need to have the 'right' emotions, and how on earth can you achieve that?

There are two ways, and one is to convince yourself. However you really feel before your presentation, tell yourself firmly that it will be a good audience, they'll be friendly and supportive, which is likely to be the case, that you've prepared first-rate information and rehearsed it thoroughly, and you look forward to sharing it with them. Say this over and over again, whether it's true or not. Human beings are very open to suggestion, even their own. Nevertheless, it's a huge advantage if you're telling yourself the truth – in other words, if you have interesting information and you have rehearsed it thoroughly.

The other way to show the right emotions is to act. Pretend that you're taking a role in a play and that the script requires you to show a cheerful, enthusiastic state of mind. So you do, no matter how you really feel. The particularly good news about this is that in producing all the right body language, you start to make the emotion true. NVC is so powerful that, at least in part, it can actually produce the feelings that themselves produce the NVC. Now you know why some good actors can cry on stage whenever tears are needed!

Eye contact

So you've walked confidently to your place and looked at the audience. That look is of enormous importance: in our culture, eye contact between speakers, or between speaker and audience, is essential. In ordinary conversation, we expect the person who's talking to us to look at us. If they don't, we start to doubt their honesty; we may even think of them as 'shifty', a word we use almost exclusively in this context. In talking to an audience, you can't afford to be seen as in any way untrustworthy, either not believing what you say or trying to hide information that your listeners might quite reasonably expect to know. However nervous you feel and however reluctant to meet the eyes of the people in front of you, you absolutely must make eye contact.

This means that you allow your eyes to meet those of other people, just for a brief instant. Don't try to avoid genuine eye contact by looking just over their heads or at their hairlines, as they will soon become aware of what you're doing. Eye contact has to be brief; if you hold it for too long, you are both likely to start laughing with embarrassment – a terrible distraction in a presentation. Of course, you can't look at everyone all of the time and, if you have a large audience, there will be some people with whom you can't make eye contact, as you may not even be able to see them clearly. The secret is to make eye contact with different people in different parts of the room, so that if a few people are missed, they will understand that you've at least tried to look in their direction.

The most difficult people to make eye contact with are those who are sitting to the immediate left and right of you as they are outside the normal arc of your vision. From time to time, turn slightly in their direction and make eye contact with them so that they don't feel left out. Don't let this become too regular, though, or you may look as if you're watching a tennis match.

The importance of making eye contact can't be overstated: it's the foundation of the trust that must exist between speaker and audience. There's an odd aspect of it, too: if you make eye contact right at the start, when you first see the audience, you're likely to go on doing so throughout your presentation; if you try to avoid it at the beginning, it will become increasingly difficult, and you may never manage to persuade the audience that they can listen to you with confidence.

Facial expression

At the start of your talk, you not only look at the audience, you smile at them. Speakers are sometimes reluctant to use facial expression in a formal setting, although they'd use it without thinking if they were talking with friends. Your expression supports your words. Try the following exercise.

Body Language Exercise 2

Try saying the following sentences, and see what happens automatically to your expression as you speak:

I do agree with what you've said.
(Did you nod your head slightly, and move it forward a tiny bit towards the person you were agreeing with?)

No, I entirely disagree.
(Did you shake your head, moving slightly away from the other person?)

It's a surprising fact.
(You probably registered surprise, raising your eyebrows and opening your eyes wider.)

What a disgusting taste!
(Did you wrinkle your face up, frown slightly and move your head back?)

In each case, you reacted instinctively to the words you were saying, so that your body language supported the meaning.

In just the same way that a friend to whom you talk socially sees and interprets your body language, the audience also recognises how you feel about what you're saying. It's difficult, but not impossible, to deceive people: try saying 'Surprising!' without looking surprised, or saying 'What a delicious pudding!' while wrinkling your face as you did for the disgusting taste: it isn't easy, is it?

Surprising!

A smile is one of the easiest and most commonly recognised signs of emotion: it suggests friendliness, contentment, shared experience – all aspects of a successful presentation. Start your rapport with the audience by smiling at them and, as we said earlier, they'll respond by smiling back.

Sitting and standing

Having smiled at the audience, you'll move to the right place and either sit or stand in order to begin to speak. Whichever you do, you need to be comfortable while looking businesslike. If you choose to sit, either because it's expected, as at a seminar, or because there's only a small audience, sit as far back in your chair as you can, thus giving yourself maximum back support. You can put your feet under the chair or together in front of you, but don't stretch your legs out and cross your feet, as this will tend to make you slide down in the chair until you look too casual, too much at ease. It may also tempt your feet to take on a life of their own, crossing and uncrossing themselves or drawing circles in the air, which may entertain but will also distract your audience. Lean slightly towards the table if you need to do so, but, if you have a script in front of you, don't hunch your shoulders forward over it; put it at the right distance for easy reading and be ready to look up at other people as often as you can.

If you choose to stand, because of the formality of the occasion, or because you have more than about a dozen people in front of you or you need to use visual aids at length (see Chapter 3), stand in a well-balanced way so that you aren't tempted to rock backwards and forwards or from side to side. This sort of regular movement can be distracting for the audience. Keep your feet a small distance apart (about 14–15 cm, depending on your height) and balance your weight equally between them. This helps you to stand firmly but not to look too stiff. Standing to attention looks odd and, unless you've been in the army and are used to it, you may find that you start to sway. Put your main weight on the heels of your feet rather than forward on your toes, and don't let either your arms or your legs become too stiff and tense. You should be standing at ease and be able to move as needed without finding that your joints have become locked into position.

NVC in the middle of your talk

You're ready to start your talk and your audience is ready to listen. For the next twenty minutes, or however long it lasts, you'll be using body language to reinforce your meaning. Sometimes it will be totally natural: you use your hand to indicate a height ('So high!'), you pick up the pointer and move back to indicate a detail on the screen, you say something mildly amusing and smile. When you aren't doing any of these things, what do you do with your hands? They present a speaker with a bit of a problem: if you wave them in the air, they can be distracting; if you put them in your pockets, you look too casual; if you fold your arms, you look defensive; if you put your fingers together to form a sort of church roof (a not uncommon habit of politicians), you look as if you might be going to preach a sermon. Clearly, none of these is desirable. Some speakers put their hands behind their back and others just let them hang loosely by their sides, but probably the easiest way to deal with them is to have something to hold: notes and a pointer are the obvious tools which you may be going to use anyway. Even if you don't need the pointer, nobody is going to worry if you hold one. This is less comfortable if you're sitting down, but then hands are less of a problem if you can keep them tidily under the table or holding your script. Don't forget that if you need to use your hands to stress a point or to show something to your audience, you need first to put down anything you're holding. Too many speakers wave a pointer in the air as if they were conducting an orchestra with it, or they cling on to the pointer and notes when they are using the remote control and end up dropping everything.

Open hands signify an outgoing nature, friendliness and sympathy with other people; a clenched fist is aggressive. As a result, if you use your hands to indicate someone, perhaps a member of the audience who wants to ask a question, always do so with your hand open, palm outstretched towards the person indicated. Don't use a finger to point (this tends to go with a clenched fist), and move your arm out from the shoulder, not just from the elbow.

Don't look as if you're conducting an orchestra

Movement

There will be moments when you want to move towards the audience. If, for example, you suggest agreement, the problem you all share, their need to use the information you're giving them, you can strengthen your words by a slight forward movement – if you're standing, take a step or two forwards. At other times, you may need to move back to the screen or turn towards people sitting at the side. These are easy, natural movements which have the effect of reinforcing your meaning, so helping to build up the essential rapport with the audience. Body language is powerful – if you say that you're happy to answer questions but you are moving backwards, your audience might well get the impression that you'd rather run away!

NVC and questions

In mentioning questions, we're clearly coming to the end of your presentation. As you receive a question look (pleasantly!) at the questioner; as you finish your answer, look at the questioner again with a smile. In between, while you are giving the answer, look round at the whole audience; this keeps them involved and helps you to continue to project your voice for everyone to hear. If your questioner sits on the front row, you can easily get into conversation with him or her, dropping your voice and forgetting that the rest of the audience wants to hear what you say. Watch how you stand, too: if you turn too far towards a questioner and forget to turn back, you may end up addressing half the audience while the other half is left out.

NVC at the end of the session

Finally, the questions are finished and you are free to sit down or sit back. Remember that you're still on view, and if you sigh with relief that it's all over, or flop back in your chair with a look of exhaustion, the audience will see this, too. What's more, as it's the last thing that they'll see you do, it's the impression they'll be left with. In a very formal and stressful presentation, such as the one you'll probably have to give in a job interview, this could be disastrous. Leave your audience with a smile and walk off in the same lively, alert way in which you appeared at the start, and both they and you will be left with a sense of a job well done.

Body Language Exercise 3

Take a rest from work and watch a news or current affairs programme on TV. As people are interviewed, look carefully at their body language and try to assess how they're feeling. In spite of their confident words, do you feel that sometimes they are tense (sitting forward stiffly, tensing their hands), or aggressive (jutting the chin forward, tensing the neck and shoulders) or hesitant in their replies (looking around slightly desperately as if for help, fidgeting)? Try to recognise these signs and interpret them. There's a problem, of course, in that some politicians have been trained to use confident body language to hide other emotions. However, sometimes you can catch them out if they relax their guard for a moment. Look, too, for genuine concern or involvement – the enthusiasm that an individual may truly feel for the message conveyed.

When you talk in public, you are showing similar NVC and your audience is watching for it too.

● Nerves

You may be thinking that the question you'd most like us to answer is how to do away with nerves before a presentation. In that case, you will be disappointed, because the single most important message about nerves is that *they are a good thing.* Be grateful for your nerves and don't try to get rid of them, especially in counterproductive ways such as drinking alcohol, which dries the throat and tends to undermine the tension that you really should be feeling.

Advantages of nerves

Why are nerves so beneficial? First, they produce a flow of adrenalin which enhances your brain power and may help you to remember information that you didn't even know you knew. The same adrenalin has another useful effect: it brightens your performance, adding an edge to it which creates a sense of excitement in your listeners and also, interestingly, in you. This is one of the reasons why students who've particularly dreaded giving a talk often say afterwards, in surprise, 'It was really quite fun, once I got going.' Your audience feels this brightness as a sense of occasion, as if they've gone to the theatre to see a well-reviewed performance and they're looking forward to it. Many of them will also be feeling grateful to you: you're speaking, so they don't have to.

The second advantage of nerves is that they help you to build a rapport with the audience. Audiences sense your nervous tension and are complimented by it. You obviously care about them and want to do well, otherwise why would you be nervous? There are, alas, other answers to this question, such as 'because you haven't prepared and rehearsed your talk properly', but if you read the following chapters, you'll know how to avoid this pitfall. Inexperienced speakers often worry about letting the audience see that they're nervous, as if there were some kind of disgrace in making the end of the pointer or your notes shake a bit. Audiences don't mind at all, as long as you remain in control. If you lose control and your nerves overwhelm you, then you embarrass them and they don't like that to happen.

Overconfidence

If you aren't nervous, you lose these advantages, and you may face another problem. It's possible to be overconfident, and if you are, this also shows. Overconfidence may mean that the speaker doesn't prepare the material sufficiently thoroughly or rehearse enough. It may also produce a casual, laid-back approach, which the audience perceives as a lack of concern for them. If they don't matter to the speaker, why should they bother to listen? Or, even more worryingly, they may take their revenge later by asking extremely difficult questions!

Controlling your nerves

You need, then, to be nervous, but not to be overcome by nerves. Obviously, the best way to achieve this is to make sure that you have plenty of good, accurate information to give, and that you've rehearsed your talk carefully with the appropriate visual aids. You must have confidence in your material and your ability to convey it to others.

Mental attitude   Having done this, make sure that you have the right frame of mind about the occasion. Ideally, a speaker should be thinking, 'Yes, I'm nervous, but I'm also confident that I can do this.' Such a mixture of nerves and confidence allows the adrenalin to flow but keeps you in control. Tell yourself, especially in the final half hour or so before your talk, that you've got good material, that you've rehearsed it well, the audience will be friendly and also impressed by what you say, and that you can make a success of this and fully intend to do so. This autosuggestion won't remove your nerves, but it's surprising how it increases your confidence.

Good breathing   Make sure that you breathe properly. In discussing ways of using your voice well (pp. 9–10), we talked about the need to breathe deeply from the diaphragm without hunching your shoulders. This is particularly important as you approach your talk, because nerves have the effect of making you raise and tense your shoulders and neck muscles. Notice, next time you're really agitated about something, how you instinctively react with your shoulders and be aware that this has a wider effect. If your shoulders are hunched, you'll tend to stiffen your arms and even clench your hands (remember that this is a sign of aggression). You may also stiffen your whole stance, so that you look as though you're on guard duty and very uncomfortable about it.

Undermine all this by freeing your shoulders. Breathe deeply a couple of times and, as you do so, shake your shoulders gently to make sure that they're relaxed, and then let your arms flop by your side. You're easing the tension in your shoulders and arms, and this will communicate itself to your whole body. You will almost immediately stand 'at ease' rather than to attention, and you'll both look and feel more comfortable. Do this again just before you appear in front of your audience.

Deep breathing has a beneficial effect on our whole being, not least on any nervous tension. While you wait to speak, take a good breath, relax your shoulders and then let the breath out slowly and in a controlled way. You can do this, if you practise, without the audience noticing anything, and you will automatically feel more confident, more in control.

There will be moments even during your talk when you can do this again. If you're waiting while the audience looks at a visual aid (they won't be looking at you), do the same little exercise; you might try it as you wait for questions, too. If there is a problem, for instance you lose your place in your notes or use the wrong visual aid, give yourself a moment to put it right in silence and, as you do so, take a deep breath and let it out in a slow, controlled way. Then forget the incident, as the audience will. If you continue to worry about it, you'll start to lose confidence; it's much better to accept that little difficulties can arise even in the best and most professional of presentations, and if you've handled it well, nobody will worry.

You're probably thinking that this chapter has given you an enormous amount of advice to absorb but that there's no way you'll remember it all when you come to make a presentation. Of course, you're absolutely right. You remember that earlier in this chapter we talked about setting up good habits, and that's what you need to do. Decide on one area of your speaking skills that you need to improve, and work at it whenever you have the chance, and especially when you're rehearsing a talk. Don't worry about it as you actually present – you'll have other things on your mind and, anyway, you'll probably find that you've set up the habit and it happens automatically. Next time, work at another aspect until that produces another good habit, and so on. You'll be surprised at how quickly you can improve your speaking techniques and, what's more, gain confidence. We said at the start of this chapter that confidence is the key to a successful presentation and that's what all this advice has been about. When you feel that you're speaking more effectively, you'll be right – you are.

Top Tips

- Prepare and rehearse thoroughly if you want to impress your audience
- Vary the volume and speed of your delivery for emphasis and interest
- Slow down and speak up, right to the end of the sentence
- Have the confidence to allow silence
- Relate to the audience right at the start by using effective body language
- Smile when appropriate and make eye contact most of the time
- Finish positively, with another smile
- Answer questions to the whole audience
- Breathe well to give yourself confidence and support your voice
- Don't worry about being nervous – it really helps! Be confident, too

3 Choosing and Using Visual Aids

This chapter helps you to

- understand the advantages of using visual aids
- avoid unclear, irrele-vant and unnecessary visual material
- choose the right moment to show your images
- design a winning visual aid: material, font colour, background
- check your visual material and rehearse with appropriate equipment
- make the most of specific visual aids such as the data projector or smartboard
- prepare demonstra-tions and posters which make an impact
- be in control of your visuals at all times

● Advantages of visual aids

Nowadays, audiences are used to seeing visual mate-rial during almost any sort of talk or presentation. Listening isn't easy and it helps a great deal if you have something to look at. In any case, human beings tend to remember what they see more readily than what they hear, and so audiences are grateful for the reinforcement of a good visual aid. People also like looking at pictures – it makes a pleasant alternative to listening – and a change in the way in which informa-tion is presented adds variety and interest to the occasion and so helps them to concentrate.

For all these reasons, audiences want visual aids and most speakers provide them. There are, no doubt, some highly experienced, witty and knowledgeable people who can hold an audience's attention by themselves, but it's probably unwise to assume that either we or you are of their number.

However, we're going to add a comment here that might surprise you. You can have too much of a good thing, and that includes visual aids. Visual aid fatigue is a recognised modern phenomenon: too many speakers either think that they can get away with lots of well-prepared visuals and not much real content or they want to 'entertain' their audience (however serious the topic under discussion) by showing all the many clever things that PowerPoint can do. All-singing, all-dancing visuals are a bore: don't try them. It's worth remembering, too, that if you are dealing with a serious scientific subject, for instance, lists of bullet points may give an oversimplified – and therefore dangerous – view of the complexity of the topic to your audience.

Having given you the warning, we'll now talk about visual aids as helpful to speaker and audience, as, of course, properly used, they are.

Visual material is prepared in advance, and if it's well-designed and thoroughly checked, it becomes an area of the presentation that the speaker doesn't have to worry about, assuming, of course, that the equipment is available and functioning properly. It also deflects attention from the speaker. This can be bad as well as good: it's possible to use so many visual aids that the audience feels that they are seeing a film or video rather than meeting and listening to a human being. As films and DVD recordings can be transported easily from one place to another, they may also feel that it was rather a waste of their time bothering to come to the venue on a particular day at a prescribed time, when they could have watched the whole thing at home at their leisure. On the other hand, many speakers like to feel that occasionally during the talk they are not the main focus of the audience's attention. This is often especially true at the beginning and is a good reason for having a visual aid containing the subject and the speaker's name to show as the presentation starts. It may also be helpful in allowing the audience to see how the speaker's name is spelt.

There are other advantages, from the speaker's point of view, in using visual aids. More detail can be shown than could possibly be explained in words: photographs will clarify aspects of the subject which couldn't be shown in any other way, and movement and sound can be included. The key message will be reinforced, and this is an advantage for the speaker just as much as for the audience.

During your course, you are likely to be using a data projector, a smartboard or possibly an overhead projector (OHP), the last of these being in a sense 'old technology' but still easy to use and transport, and so still popular on some courses. We'll look at these later in this chapter, together with some of the other forms of visual information that you might need to use, such as handouts, posters and demonstrations. Incidentally, you may hear people refer to a presentation using computer-generated visual material and a data projector as a 'PowerPoint presentation', even if the computer package they're using isn't Microsoft and so isn't PowerPoint. It's just become the general term, in the same way that people call a vacuum cleaner a 'hoover', whatever make it is. However, before we get into the details of the equipment you're going to use, we need to look at when and where you might use visual aids of any sort, and what you need to remember in preparing them.

● Using visual aids

Inappropriate visual aids

Are there any times when visual aids are not a good idea? We've mentioned the problem of using too many, so that the speaker and the message are overwhelmed by the visual material. Poor-quality visuals are distracting and let down the whole occasion: people are used to high-definition, broadcast-quality visual material and are disappointed if they are offered anything less. This is especially true of visual aids which are so unclear that they fail to convey any message at all. If photographs are under- or over-exposed, colours look indistinct or the print is too small (see p. 38), the visual aid will fail to make the right impact and will leave the audience wishing that the speaker had been more aware of their needs. Irrelevant visuals are even worse. Occasionally, speakers feel that they can 'cheer up' a difficult or potentially boring subject by showing pictures which are pleasant to look at but not in any way relevant to the message. At worst, these can even be childishly humorous. This is clearly unprofessional and profoundly irritating to an audience that has taken time and trouble to come to hear a serious subject discussed.

As visual aids are so important, there's sometimes a feeling amongst inexperienced presenters that every point made has to be shown on the screen. This can result not only in too many, but also in unnecessary and rather patronising visual aids: a real-life example is of a group of management students who discussed the results of a questionnaire they'd carried out. 'About a quarter of people said yes', they explained, 'and about three-quarters said no.' This was clear enough, but on the screen appeared a pie chart, with two segments, showing one-quarter and three-quarters in different colours, with a key underneath. The intention was a good one, but there's no need for a visual aid if the point has already been made and understood.

When to use a visual aid

The decision about if and when to use a visual aid depends to a certain extent on the occasion and the constraints imposed by the situation. If you're reading a seminar paper, for instance, you're likely to be sitting at a table surrounded by the group, and it may be quite difficult to leave your place and move to a data projector or an OHP; there's also the probability that everyone won't be able to see the screen easily: people to your right and left will have to move their chairs back and round in order to see. You need to decide whether all this movement is worthwhile. You may feel that it is, in which case you should make sure in advance that the equipment is set up and the chairs are placed so that there's the minimum disruption. If you have several visual aids to show, you might want to group them, if possible, so that the interruption happens only once. You may decide that a handout, with a copy for each person, is much easier to use than a screen-based visual aid.

On the other hand, a seminar presentation, when the presentation techniques themselves are being assessed as well as the treatment of the subject, might well be an occasion for using a number of visual aids. If you are studying science or engineering, you will almost certainly rely heavily on visual aids, and you will be assessed on these as well as on other aspects of your work. A poster presentation, for instance, will involve you in the design and use of high-quality posters (see pp. 57–9), while a project presentation will require you to illustrate your work regularly throughout your talk. We'll discuss this in more detail later.

However, there are some points in most presentations at which a visual aid is appropriate. Some of these occasions are more common in arts-based and others in science and technology-based subjects, but the division isn't absolute, of course, and this list certainly isn't exhaustive:

- An introductory slide, showing your name(s), the title of your talk and the date. This makes a useful introduction and gives the audience something to look at as you start. You may wish to repeat this introductory slide at the end of your session.
- An outline of your talk. This is likely to be a list of points, either numbered or bulleted, which the audience can note in order to have an overview of what you are going to say.
- A general view before you look at the detail. This would apply to a slide of a painting, a management hierarchy chart, a building site or an electronic circuit block diagram.
- Detail which you're going to discuss, and which the audience needs to see in order to be able to follow what you say. This could, for instance, be a line of poetry, a bar of music, a small part of a painting, a line drawing of a component or the seed of a plant under a microscope. Sometimes, such details may be too small to be seen in the normal way by the naked eye.
- Movement which you need to describe. This might be the growth pattern of a tree or the possible spread of fire through a building. The data projector (see pp. 46–9) is particularly good at showing such development.
- Relationships which you need to discuss. This might involve a family tree, a flow chart or a map of a country showing population distribution or climate change.
- Simple mathematical material, such as a table of figures or a graph. However, if such material becomes complex, it ceases to be useful as a visual aid.

Visual aids preliminary checklist

You are preparing a presentation and trying to decide which visual aids you will use. Consider the following:

- ❏ What equipment is available?
- ❏ Do you know how to order it and, if necessary, collect it and set it up?
- ❏ What visual aids will other speakers be using?
- ❏ Is the room suitable for visual aids, in terms of size, lighting, blinds, etc?
- ❏ How long is your talk? This will to a certain extent dictate the number of visual aids you use.
- ❏ If you are using a data projector or an OHP, what colours will you use for background, lettering and so on? Will you have a coloured background?
- ❏ Will you have an introductory slide, with your subject and your name on it?
- ❏ Will you show a bullet-point list of the contents of your talk?
- ❏ At which points of your presentation will you and the audience need to see a diagram or other illustration?
- ❏ Do you want a summary slide at the end?
- ❏ Allow at least twenty seconds per slide; how will this affect the amount of information you can give the audience?
- ❏ Do you need to reproduce any of your slides as handouts to give to the audience or the person marking the assignment?
- ❏ If your chosen equipment fails, what will you use as back-up? This is particularly important if you're using a data projector or smartboard.

Designing a visual aid

Whatever form of visual aid you choose, there's one overriding criterion: everyone in the audience must be able to see everything you show. This sounds obvious, but inexperienced speakers sometimes crowd their material on the screen, whether it's words or diagrams, until it's impossible for the audience to see the details. Let's look first at the potential problems of words and then at punctuation, colour and backgrounds.

Font size and style There isn't space on a screen for many words if they're a sensible size for viewing. In a seminar room, you can probably use a font of about 20 point and the audience will be able to read the words; in a large lecture theatre, you may need 26 or 30 point. This means, incidentally, that it isn't wise to copy or scan printed material: almost certainly, the print size will be 12 point, far too small to be read even by people sitting near the front. There's also likely to be too much on the page. Look at a typical page from a textbook or a report. It has hundreds of words and also irrelevant details such as a page number. The most important sentence on the page might come down near the bottom, where it would hardly be noticed if it were projected. If there's a diagram on the page, it will be small, with a label that might be 10 point italic. It isn't sensible to try to use such a page as a visual aid, although it happens more often than you would expect.

There's another consideration, which is the style of font you choose. If you look at one of the most common fonts for documents, Times New Roman, you'll see that the letters are smaller than in some other fonts and have serifs, the small extra strokes or curls at the edges of the letters. These help the reading and look attractive on the page. However, a visual aid needs to be as simple and uncluttered as possible, so a sanserif font, in which the letters don't have serifs, is clearer when it's projected. Arial is a good choice. You may want to make a heading look more interesting by using 'shadowed' or outline letters, or a more elaborate font. Be careful! It's easy to make your visual aid harder to read, or even oddly childish, by overdoing such techniques. Generally speaking, for your headings use large bold capitals in the font you're using already, perhaps in a different colour from the rest of the text, and they will stand out sufficiently.

It's perhaps unwise to suggest a maximum number of words on the screen at any one time, as it must depend on the purpose of the visual aid and the size of the room in which it's shown, but twenty-five is a reasonable number to use as a guideline. This might include four or five words used as a heading, and the rest as a list of points underneath. Bulleted points are usually better than numbered, as they make more visual impact, although there are times, of course, when numbers are needed. If you need to use them, don't add brackets or full stops: the numbers by themselves will be clear enough if they're well spaced and, again, you want to avoid clutter.

Selecting the words Try not to use full sentences on the screen and never show a long paragraph of writing. You are producing visual material, not a written text, and you must therefore show only what the audience can read easily, which means the minimum of words necessary to give the message. For instance, suppose you are a history student, and have been asked to give a seminar about the revival of monasticism in the Middle Ages, focusing on the Abbey of Cluny. You might want to give your group the following information in visual form to reinforce your message:

> *The Abbey Church of Cluny was founded in 1088. It was the largest*
> *Romanesque building in Western Europe, and its architecture and*
> *decoration were enormously influential. It became immensely rich*
> *and politically powerful, because of its independence and the eminence*
> *and capability of its abbots.*

There are 45 words in this paragraph, far too many to put on the screen. This doesn't matter, though, as you are going to tell your audience the details, and all you need to show them are bullet points to focus their attention. You could use a heading with a list of points under it, as shown below.

Abbey Church of Cluny
Founded 1088

- Huge size and fine architecture
- Capable, influential abbots
- Enormous wealth
- Independence and political power

You now have just 19 words and one date on the screen, so you can use a sensible style and size of font in order to project these key ideas. You will be able to enlarge on these details as you talk, for instance explaining the nature and extent of the influence of the Abbey of Cluny, and the audience will be able to use your bullet points as headings in their notes and fill in as much detail as they think is appropriate. You'll see that you have identified the most important words for your audience, so they can concentrate on what you say rather than having to worry about exactly what your message might be. These are important aspects of the speaker's responsibility: clarifying issues and highlighting key ideas for those who listen (see also p. 16).

Punctuation   You'll also have noticed that there's no punctuation in the visual aid version of the example above, although the original passage has normal full stops and commas. Very little punctuation is needed on a visual aid, partly because there won't often be complete sentences and partly because we're simplifying and removing anything which might be thought of as 'clutter' (not that, in ordinary writing, punctuation isn't an integral and essential part of the way in which an author conveys meaning). A few punctuation marks should be used if they're appropriate, for instance a direct question that isn't followed by a question mark always looks wrong, and apostrophes should be used correctly in the normal way. On the other hand, a list doesn't have to be introduced by a colon, and it's rare to need commas unless they affect the meaning of the words. So leave punctuation out unless the result looks odd or is ambiguous. Otherwise, you might produce something like this:

In our test, we used the following equipment:-

(1) an oscilloscope;
(2) a digital voltmeter;
(3) a signal generator;
(4) a logic analyser;
(5) power supplies;
(6) a soldering iron.

The above visual aid is both wordy and overpunctuated. There is no point in numbering items in a list if their order is, as here, irrelevant, and the repetition of 'a' or 'an' is unnecessary and irritating. The speaker will introduce the list by saying that the team used this equipment, and so there is no point in saying so on the screen. Even in a printed document, the final semicolons would be left out nowadays – the individual items in the list are so short that they don't need artificial separation in this way. A cluttered slide such as this one will appear messy on the screen, and the important information, the words, will take longer to identify and read. An improved version, which will be perfectly clear to the audience, might be like this:

Equipment

- oscilloscope
- digital voltmeter
- signal generator
- logic analyser
- power supplies
- soldering iron

Colour on the screen Whatever form of visual aid equipment you are using, you may choose to have a coloured background and a contrasting colour for the text or diagram. Plain black text on a clear base will be sufficient under some circumstances, such as a seminar paper in which you're showing half a dozen bullet points, but for any occasion in which your presentation skills themselves are important, you'll certainly need to use colour if you want your work to have a professional appearance.

You have a choice between using a dark colour for the background and a light colour for text, or doing the opposite: you may be simply trying to achieve a strong contrast. In practice, it's a bit more complicated. It's essential that the contrast between background and text (or diagrammatic material) is sufficient, but this isn't always clear from the computer screen. Unless you project your image on a large screen, as you will during your presentation, you can't be sure that your colour choice will work. This is especially true if you use two shades of the same colour: dark blue text on a light blue background can be effective, but you need to project it to be sure that the letters stand out clearly. You also need to make sure that your colours look pleasant together and, again, it's hard to be sure unless you see them on a large screen. Clashing colours, or an unpleasant mix, will distract the audience from important information. A popular colour choice is a dark blue background with white or yellow for the text: this works well and looks attractive. Once you've chosen your basic colour scheme, don't depart from it without a good reason. The colour you show has to mean something to your audience: if, for example, you use dark blue for background with yellow for main headings and white for the rest of your text, the audience will very quickly get used to this pattern. If you then use other colours, they will ask themselves why. If the answer's clear (for instance you want to highlight a particular number in a small table), they will accept it, but if it isn't, the question can become a major distraction.

Consistency is also important, especially if you're part of a group presentation. If one of you uses red for a particular section of a map, for instance, then everyone who shows the same area must use red. In the same way, be consistent yourself and agree a consistent format between the members of the group in such details as the style of headings and the colour of the border if you use one.

Colour can cause problems, too, for the high percentage of men who have some colour deficiency in their sight. Obviously, you can't make allowances for the small number who are totally colour blind, but there are some combinations which often present difficulty and which you need to avoid: red and green is the most common. Blue and black, or yellow and brown, are safer combinations. Such problems of colour recognition are, oddly, rare among women, although not unknown.

Some colours simply don't show up well: pink and orange are in this category, while green can look faded and needs to be used with care. A patch of red is effective, but writing or fine line drawing in red simply doesn't project sufficiently strongly. This is not what you'd expect, red being a bright and dramatic colour in itself. As a result, people use, say, black for the text and then highlight the key words in red, only to find that the words they wanted to emphasise show much less strongly than their surroundings. Black always projects well, with dark blue almost as good, and brown and purple are generally easy to see.

Once you have a colour combination you're happy with, you can use it whenever you like. If you're using PowerPoint, you can copy your master slide with its colours into a new presentation, and you have your chosen colours readily available. This can have a useful side effect. We'll say something later about the need for back-up (see pp. 48–9), but if you regularly create presentations with the same colours, you may be able to reuse some of your slides from a previous occasion, as they'll match your new ones.

Backgrounds We've discussed background colours above, but you may like the look of some of the patterned backgrounds available on PowerPoint or similar packages. They need to be chosen carefully, in the light of your main message. Unless you're talking about life on a tropical island, waving palm trees in the background are just as inappropriate as humour in a serious subject.

Some standard backgrounds contain their own traps for the indiscriminate user. If, for example, you choose one which is pale in colour at the top and progressively darker down the screen, you're faced with a quandary: do you use light coloured print, which disappears at the top but shows up well lower down, or a dark print that looks splendid at the top but is hardly visible towards the bottom? If you feel that you've found a colour that works for the whole image, have you allowed for the fact that a diagram may look unbalanced, some sections apparently highlighted while other sections are very pale?

Unintended emphasis can occur with any background that has patterns on it. A popular example is an attractive dark blue with a red bar about two-thirds of the way down on the left-hand side. This stretches about a third of the way across the screen. If the speaker happens to have a word or a number just above this line, it appears to be underlined in red. If the word or

In England the Black Death in 1348 Killed one and a half million people.

Avoid humour in a serious subject

number happens to be over the red bar, it may be less clear than other words and numbers on the screen – and the viewer will wonder why.

The overall advice that comes out of a discussion of backgrounds is that, on the whole, a plain colour is safest, and the more technical or scientific the content of your image, the more important it is that nothing should distract from it or distort its message.

Visual aids checklist

Take any one of your visual aids, project it and test it in the light of the following questions. Before you give your presentation, check all your visual aids this way:

❑ If a colleague stands at the back of the room, can he or she see every detail on the screen?

❑ Is there material which is irrelevant and should be removed (such as a slide number or the source of a diagram)?

❑ Does the slide need to be corrected (for instance because of a spelling error) or updated (for instance because a statistic has been superseded)?

❑ Is there unnecessary punctuation on the slide?

❑ Has any essential punctuation been left out?

❑ Is the colour combination pleasing to look at?

❑ Has the message been distorted because of the background or layout of the slide?

❑ Is every diagram correctly and clearly labelled?

❑ Have you shown more detail than the audience can easily follow?

❑ Is all the lettering big enough to be easily read?

❑ Are there too many words on the screen?

❑ Have you shown long sentences or paragraphs which are difficult to read?

❑ Is this slide consistent in style and layout with any others that you will use?

❑ Overall, is your message clear, easy to understand and attractively presented?

● **Visual aid equipment**

Nowadays, you are likely to use one of three types of visual aid equipment: the data projector, operated from a computer (often a laptop) through the projector itself onto a screen, a smartboard (sometimes called an interactive whiteboard) and the more old-fashioned OHP, with diagrams which are printed onto the appropriate form of acetate. Hand-drawn overhead slides are of course unacceptable nowadays. There are other forms of visual aid, such as handouts and demonstrations, which we'll discuss later in the chapter.

Before you spend time and effort preparing visual aid material, check with your tutor or lecturer to make sure that you know exactly what is appropriate. Is the assignment assessed and, if so, is the visual content evaluated as part of that assessment? How many images are you likely to show? If there are only one or two, it might be better to give handouts than to use complex technology. Do you have to arrange your own equipment or will the lecturer provide it for you? If you book it yourself, how much notice should you give? Remember, too, that you need to have the equipment available for rehearsal as well as for the performance.

Adequate rehearsal is essential. Too often, people practise the talk itself, but leave preparation of the visuals until the last minute; they may even look slightly surprised in front of the audience when they see the final version on the screen for the first time. You need to know exactly what the projected image looks like and where to find the detail, so that you can use the pointer easily as you indicate on the screen what the audience should be looking at. (They can, of course, manage text perfectly easily without help, which is why you don't need to point to words.) It's difficult for an audience to find their way through a complex image without assistance, and the pointer gives such help, if it's well used. Don't rush this: it will take people a few seconds to adjust to the image and see where the pointer is – if you simply point and remove the pointer immediately, they won't have enough time. Let the tip of the pointer rest for a moment or two on the detail that's important, then remove it. If you use a laser pointer, it's even harder for the audience to identify the point of light, especially if the image itself is multicoloured. It's difficult to keep the light steady, too. Unless the screen is too high for you to reach, you will find that the old-fashioned metal pointer is easier to use, both for you and the audience.

We've stressed pointing on the screen. If you try to use the pointer on an OHP, you will inevitably move forward and block someone's view. You will also have a bright light in your eyes, which is uncomfortable, and you won't be able to see clearly when you face the audience again. Stand back, almost alongside the screen, and you should still be able to see the image you're presenting while at the same time keeping contact with the people in front of you. A useful guide is to realise that, for most of any talk, your feet should be pointing towards the audience. If they are, you'll be facing the people you're talking to. There will be times when your feet will move round 90 degrees, so that you are sideways on to the audience, for instance when you're using material on the screen, but as soon as you've finished working through the words or diagram there, make sure that your feet turn again to their usual position and you are once more facing your audience.

Visual aids are important to any speaker, but they mustn't detract from you, the person the audience has come to see and hear. They need careful preparation and their use has to be planned and rehearsed. We'll look at the most common forms of visual aid equipment in turn.

The data projector

In recent years, the data projector has outstripped its rivals and become the standard visual aid equipment in industry and commerce in the UK. Interestingly, this trend is showing signs of being reversed: visual aids produced and shown in this way have often been poorly constructed and unappealing in use. We have all seen cartoon figures, fussy backgrounds or explosive changes of image, and heard loud and distracting music when we wanted to concentrate on the message the speaker was presenting to us. As a result of this sort of thing, people are reacting against the use of the data projector and even reverting to presentations without the support of visual aids. If you are an experienced, highly knowledgeable and proficient presenter, you may get away with this, but for most occasions, visual aids are necessary to support you and to clarify the details for the audience. Remember if you are making a presentation at a job interview to check what is expected of you – what type of visual aids or perhaps none at all.

So what are the advantages of using the data projector? We'll look at them before we start discussing the potential problems:

- You can use one piece of equipment to show text, diagrams, movement, video, even to play music if you want to; you don't need to struggle with several sources of visual image at the same time.
- It's quick and easy to change the image: you only need to click the remote control or touch the keyboard.
- You can build up an image step by step, or highlight the aspect you're talking about.
- The equipment itself is relatively small, especially if you have a ceiling-mounted projector and use a laptop; it isn't likely to get in the way of the audience as an OHP often does.
- You can update your material at any time. While you need to rehearse with your visual aids before your talk, a last-minute change or correction is possible.
- Your visual material will look professional.

These are major advantages, but there are associated problems which ought also to be kept in mind:

- Just because you can use so many types of support material, don't feel that you have to. There's a great temptation, especially when you start to use PowerPoint, to produce an 'all singing, all dancing' display which is distracting and irritating to the audience. Use movement, music and so on only if it helps you to make your point.

- It's easy to change the image, and easy to do so by accident, especially if you're nervous. If you cling on to the remote control, you may move on to the next image without even knowing that you've done so. It may be wise to leave the control on the table until you need it.

- Lists can be built up one stage at a time, but not all lists should be treated in this way. It's often better to show all the points at once, to give an overall impression. Build up a list only if doing so helps the audience's understanding.

- The equipment is small, but it's brightly lit and coloured. Don't be tempted to look at the screen of your laptop as you talk – you can end up by talking to it instead of to the audience. If you want to check the image, glance at the big screen. You might choose to switch off the laptop screen or 'blank' it while you're talking.

- It's useful to be able to change your visual aid if you discover a spelling error or want to update a statistic, but don't be tempted to make small changes for the sake of making changes. You need to rehearse with your material so that you're really familiar and at ease with it when you give your talk. You could also regret a last-minute change when you see it projected.

There are other aspects of using the data projector which you need to think about. When you prepare your material, you may find that you will be speaking for a few minutes without needing a visual aid. Include a 'blank' slide at this point, so that the audience sees just your background colour. It isn't a good idea to keep showing a slide that's become irrelevant, but you can't switch off the projector as you would an OHP. The blank slide is also useful at the end of your presentation when you ask for questions; if you simply leave the final image on the screen, questions may focus on that rather than earlier aspects of the talk, or it may become a distraction to the audience. Have a printout of your whole slide show available for your own reference, so that if you need to go back to a particular image in order to show it again, you can identify it quickly.

You may, incidentally, be asked to produce copies of your slide material as handouts, or it may seem to you to be a good idea. It rarely is, for two reasons. First, you are going to talk through your visual aids, explaining them and developing the detail further in what you say. As a result, the slide by itself, without your spoken words, may mean very little to anyone who sees it. Secondly, you may, for the same reason, be tempted to put too much on the slide, so that, while it's informative as a handout, it isn't satisfactory as a visual aid. Handouts and slides represent different ways of giving an audience supporting material; they do different jobs and should be prepared separately in the light of their specific requirements.

Although you'll prepare and rehearse your talk with care, you might still need to use the data projector's hidden slide facility that allows you to skip a slide without the audience's knowledge. This can be useful if you're running short of time, but you will give the game away if you visibly number the slides. We remember a presentation in which the images were numbered 1/17, 2/17, and so on. The speaker ran out of time and so stopped at 15/17, and inevitably the first question was, 'What didn't we see on slides 16 and 17?' In the same way, if you date each slide and then give the presentation a second time, make sure that you change the dates.

You can show the development of your subject in a way that would be difficult without a data projector, but if, for example, you show the growth of a plant or winds circulating over the south Atlantic, you must do so in silence, allowing your audience time to watch the process before you begin to discuss it.

Speed is one of the major problems of a computer-generated presentation. Speakers often forget that the images shown (such as a three-dimensional picture of a piece of equipment) can be complex, and yet it's very easy to move on. Don't be pushed by your own visual material into speaking more quickly or showing the slides more rapidly than you intended. Taking your time is a mark of an experienced and confident presenter.

You will, however, have to be aware of the audience's perception of time. For example, there's a limit to how long the audience will sit waiting for your presentation to start. It takes at least two or three minutes to boot up the computer and set up the presentation, and if you're using unfamiliar equipment, you may find yourself becoming increasingly agitated as you check cables and press keys and nothing happens. You have to make the tricky decision about how long you can go on trying to get an image on the screen before the audience gets restless. There can come a point at which you simply admit defeat and turn to your own back-up material.

Back-up is essential for computer-generated visual aids. A great deal can go wrong with the equipment itself, the software or its compatibility. In a presentation one of us saw recently, there was a sudden power cut so that a talk which depended heavily on its visual images had to be given without any. Decide in advance what type of back-up you need and make sure it's available. The OHP is probably the most common form and the easiest to use. If you print out your images onto acetate and take them with you, you can almost certainly change to this form of visual aid without much difficulty, even if you have to sacrifice some movement in doing so. At least your visuals are still good quality and attractive to look at. If you're talking to a small group, you may choose to make hard copies of your visual material and, in an emergency such as a power cut, give them out as handouts.

If you find yourself in this uncomfortable position, keep calm. The audience is likely to know about the problem and will be sympathetic, as long as they aren't kept waiting too long before the talk goes ahead. Plan in advance how you will handle the situation and put your solution into operation with a confident smile and quick apology to the audience – they will be impressed by your professionalism. Once you are under way, forget the problem: it's not good for your own confidence to keep thinking of it, and you certainly don't want to remind the audience.

Whatever form of visual material you're using, always check it carefully. A spelling error on the screen attracts and holds the audience's attention, so they forget they're supposed to be listening to what you say. Words that don't fit on to the screen and so end up on the wall or ceiling aren't easy to read and suggest that you didn't rehearse with your visual material. Never use an image for which you need to apologise: if it isn't clear, get a better version or leave it out. Your visual aids need to support you, not undermine your presentation.

Personal Response System

A PRS is based on a PowerPoint presentation and so it's worth looking at it here. We have to say at once that it isn't easy to use effectively as part of a presentation and that a great deal of careful preparation and practice is needed! It can also be used as a gimmick to impress an audience rather than because their instant opinion is important, and this will be extremely irritating to those involved.

The idea behind a PRS is that you can ask an audience to respond immediately to what you are saying, using PRS units ('clickers'). In creating your presentation, you will be prompted to choose whether a particular slide is to offer the audience a question (multiple choice, true or false, survey answer, etc.). If you do this, you will at that point of your talk have to allow time for the audience to answer by using their clickers (you can set the system to allow a fixed amount of time for this if you wish to do so); the system will then present the answers on the screen in any format that you have chosen.

PRS can be used in different ways. You may be producing answers for immediate use so that you can gauge the understanding of the audience or find their reaction to what you have said or to an issue that you have raised. On the other hand, you may be collecting the responses to evaluate later or to feed into a subsequent presentation.

As with all technology, you will need to make sure that the equipment is available and in working order and you will have to allow time to set it all up before you start. This is one of the problems. The system has to recognise *your* group and to be set up to record the answers in the form that you want, and this can take time. To do all this in front of an audience could be a horrible experience, especially if they haven't used clickers before and are feeling a bit apprehensive. It isn't hard for members of the audience to be involved with PRS, but they might be nervous about the type of questions they will be asked.

Your most important preparation is the decision about *why* you want to use PRS. It can enliven a talk, encourage audience involvement and give you instant feedback, but you must be sure that you want to achieve these goals on this particular occasion. If, for instance, you are studying politics and have been introducing your audience to the different forms of proportional representation that might be used in the UK, you might want to use PRS in two stages: initially to find out how many of your colleagues think that the current first-past-the-post system should be changed and then, later, to assess whether there is a clear majority in favour of a particular form of proportional representation. This could make your talk more immediate and more lively, ensuring that your audience felt that their opinion was important and that your work was seen as directly connected to a current point of view.

On the other hand, the use of PRS could interrupt the audience's concentration, or indeed your own. If you are taking them through a complex scientific experiment, the last thing you need is for the audience to be startled into making a decision about, for example, the ethical aspects of what you are describing. Beware of using PRS casually; make sure that it will add to the quality of your talk and that you have tried the system out on your friends and feel confident that you can use it effectively and with the minimum of disruption. Ideally, you should have been at one or two events where it has been used by other speakers so that you can see how it can be embedded in a talk without interfering with the flow of the presentation itself. Then you might want to try it out when the subject is appropriate to see how it can add to your own presentation skills.

The smartboard (interactive whiteboard)
The great advantage of a smartboard is that it combines the convenience and spontaneity of a flipchart with the high quality and professionalism of a data projector. Smartboards are known by different names and their functions vary

with different manufacturers, but their fundamental principle is the same. They have two basic functions: PowerPoint and a scrapbook.

In PowerPoint mode, you can use the smartboard just as you would an ordinary data projector, but you have the possibility of drawing on and annotating your slides. If you intend to do this, copy your PowerPoint file first, so that if you need to use it again, it isn't covered with notes from an earlier occasion. As with any data projector, you can interpose blank slides while the points you've made previously are discussed.

The second function you have available is the scrapbook, which presents you with a series of blank pages, as few or as many as you need, which you can use as if they were sheets of paper on a flipchart, but which you can save so that they form a permanent record. If, for example, you were giving a seminar presentation or leading a seminar discussion, you could prepare your talk as a PowerPoint slide show, as usual, but you could switch to scrapbook mode and make notes for the audience as the discussion developed. This is particularly useful if you are asked to distribute notes after the event.

If, for example, you were discussing a poem in a seminar presentation, you could produce the whole poem on your first PowerPoint-style smartboard slide as you read it aloud to the group. Then you could have each verse on a separate slide, and this would allow you to write on the slide, pointing out the rhyme scheme, rhythm and punctuation used by the poet. Perhaps the seminar group isn't clear about a term you use: switch to the notebook and write out the explanation just as you would on a flipchart. After the seminar, you could print out the annotated slides and the notebook pages, or distribute them electronically to the group, so that each of them had a record of the seminar.

Typing up handwritten notes later allows you to expand on the information you recorded during the talk, making a document that will be of use to those who were present and also, of course, to those who were not. It's simple to transfer your notes into your institution's virtual learning environment (BlackBoard, for example) so that your work becomes a permanent part of the archive of your course.

It's worth noting that there is software available which will automatically transform your handwriting into typed text, but at present this is not very successful and it's probably wiser to go back to your handwritten notes and type them up later for general circulation.

Most smartboards look like normal data projection screens, and you will be using a pen – which looks like a bulky biro – to prompt the system to act. You can touch the screen with the pen to switch from PowerPoint to the scrapbook and you can also decide what sort of annotation you want to create: you can highlight or erase, produce arrows, and so on. As you are using the pen each time, it will soon become familiar to you and you will be at ease with the smart-board operation. It may all sound and indeed look daunting, but it's really quite a simple communication tool once you've had some practice with it.

In terms of presentation techniques, the only aspect of using a smart-board that is different from using a flipchart is where you stand. A flipchart allows you only a small area to cover and so a right-handed person will tend to stand to their left of the flipchart in order to write naturally. In comparison to a flipchart, a smartboard is huge, and you won't be able to write on it without blocking the view of your audience for the few minutes during which you're writing. You must as a result make sure that you let your audience see a clear view of the whole screen in between annotations. Step right away from the smartboard and allow time and silence for the audience to see what you've written and, if appropriate, to make notes.

The overhead projector

The OHP is the good old-fashioned, low-technology standby among visual aid equipment. It has great advantages: it's easy to prepare the material and little can go wrong while you're using it. You may be familiar with the OHP from lectures, as it's more flexible for teaching and training than the data projector, which is much more commonly used in presentations. Recently, the OHP has made a bit of a comeback, just because it's so easy and flexible. It's also a very good back-up if you're using more advanced technology in a place you're not familiar with and something might go wrong.

There are two ways of making transparencies for the OHP: you can photo-copy from your source directly onto acetate or you can print directly on to acetate from your computer, in both cases being sure to use the right type of acetate.

As we said earlier, using printed material and photocopying it isn't usually sensible, as the details, especially letters or figures on a diagram, will be too small. You might be able to enlarge the diagram sufficiently, but it's likely that some aspects will still not be visible at the back of the room. It's much easier and safer to make your transparencies by producing the material on the computer and then printing them onto acetate. You can then design your image freely, making sure that lettering and colours are used appropriately. Even with such a simple form of visual aid, it's important to think of the audience and its needs. If you switch on the OHP with no acetate in place, the resulting bright glare will be uncomfortable for the audience and they will look away. Always put the acetate on the projector before you switch on, glancing quickly at the screen to make sure that the image isn't crooked or badly positioned.

Some projectors will produce fringe glare or distortion at the edges of the image, or the image may be in focus at one point of the screen and out of focus elsewhere. Use the controls to correct this as far as possible, and think about repositioning the projector or the screen. You may also have the problem of 'keystoning', when the image is wider at the top than the bottom. This can usually, but not always, be corrected by changing the angle of the screen. A noisy projector fan may also be a nuisance and you need to ensure that you can be heard in spite of it – this may be a good reason for switching off the projector if you aren't going to use it for a while. Don't assume that you need to switch it off whenever you change your acetate. If you do this, you may blow the bulb, and in any case it's distracting to your audience. The best guideline is to switch it off if you aren't going to show the next image for a few moments but to leave it on if you're moving on to the next acetate almost immediately. If for some reason you don't want to switch the projector off, use a 'cover' acetate which shows just the background you're using and perhaps the title of your talk as a reminder.

It's as well to check the position of the screen, especially in sunny weather. The OHP can stand quite strong light (more so than the data projector), but sunshine falling on the screen is disastrous. If you're in front of an audience for a long presentation, it's wise to check that the sun won't move round on to the screen during your talk, or draw the blinds before you start.

You may have seen your lecturers reveal the image gradually, often by putting a sheet of paper over part of the acetate. There's sometimes a benefit in doing so when you're teaching, but many students, and others, dislike the technique and find it patronising. It would be unwise to use it in a presentation. If you need to build up your image, use overlays of acetate.

As with any form of visual aid, give the audience time to assimilate the image before you start to talk about it. This takes longer than you might expect. Allow 20–30 seconds of silence, depending on the complexity of the image, before you speak. Watch the audience: their eyes will be on the screen while they're studying the image, and when they look at you again, it's safe to continue.

If you follow the guidelines about font and colour, and allow the audience the opportunity to look at and assimilate your visual material, you shouldn't have many problems with the OHP.

We've now looked at the principal forms of visual aid you're likely to use, but it's worth spending a little while on some of the others.

● Handouts

We mentioned handouts earlier in the context of the failure of your computer-generated material, but they're useful in their own right. The images on the screen may be forgotten, but the paper the audience takes away at the end remains with them and can be a constant reminder of what you said. If your role is a 'selling' one, for instance if you're a management student and you're introducing a possible career choice to your peers, or an engineering student 'selling' a device that you and your group have designed and built, it's impressive to give your audience a handout showing the main attractions of the career and any possible contacts, or a photograph of your product with the key points of its specification and its benefits to the user. This will reinforce the impact of the presentation itself and ensure that the good impression you gave at the time lasts beyond the duration of the talk. You might choose to pass round this handout before you start, or at the end of your talk, as a reminder of your main message.

Sometimes in a presentation, you need to give the audience supporting information which isn't appropriate within the talk itself. You might need to discuss the overall price of your product, but the details of how that price is made up are difficult to take in just by hearing them and not immediately relevant to what you're saying. This is handout material. Similarly, if you're describing an aspect of climate change, you might have a great many statistics available, covering many years, but all you can sensibly show to the audience is a simple graph of the trend. If they need to be able to refer to the figures, put them onto a handout and use the graph on the screen. This has the advantage that you can refer to the detailed statistics, for instance in answer to a question, and everybody can see them easily, which they certainly couldn't if you tried to project all the figures. This type of handout has to be given out before the presentation starts, so that the audience sees what you are going to discuss and can follow the detail, if necessary, on their own copies while you use the screen.

Generally, it isn't wise to give handouts to the audience during your talk, as it causes too much delay and disruption, although if you have a small number of people, fewer than ten or so, you might take the risk. Otherwise, give out the material before you start, when it's easy to check that everyone can see a copy. Just occasionally, you might want to give the audience the handouts at the end of the presentation, as a reminder of what you've said. If you do this, let them know in your introduction that this will happen, so that they don't have the frustration of writing notes only to be given the information in printed form later.

The handout must be as professional as the rest of the presentation. Design it as effectively as you can, without overcrowding the page, and make sure that each member of the audience can see a copy. Ideally, they would have a copy each, but with a student audience you might get away with one copy between two or even three – paper is expensive!

Handout checklist

You feel that it would be appropriate to use handouts for your talk. Make sure they are as effective as possible by using the following guidelines:

❑ Know exactly why you are using each handout and when it's appropriate to give it to the audience.

❑ Design your handouts so that they look as professional as possible. Avoid putting too much information or too many diagrams on one page.

❑ If you have several handouts, number them for easy reference.

❑ Check the number of people you are expecting and make sure that everyone will be able to see the handouts.

● Prototypes and demonstrations

If you're studying a technical or scientific subject, you may need to build a prototype of what you have designed and use it in your presentation. This can be very effective, but you need to plan with great care how you are going to show it to your audience.

How many people will be looking at your prototype? If you have a small audience, they may all be able to see easily, but if you have a large audience, the chances are that they will mostly get a general idea but be unable to see the details. Can you use a platform or place the prototype on a table above the level on which you're standing so that people have a better view? It might still be worth having a large picture of the product on the screen, maybe rotating it so it can be seen from all angles, in order for people to see the general shape of the prototype and then study it further by using the image on the screen.

People don't like being asked to look and listen at the same time, so when you show them your prototype, they will want to have a good look before you discuss it. If it's small enough, hold it up and turn it round very slowly in your hand, moving from side to side if necessary in order to let everyone see it. At this stage, don't continue to talk. Only when they've all had the chance to look at the prototype can you start to discuss it again. If it's too big for you to hold up, display it as well as you can, if possible from different angles. Take care not to block the view yourself; stand well to the side or behind it.

When the audience has looked at your product, then you can describe it. Indicate each part clearly and slowly with either your hand or a pointer and then speak. Pause before moving on to the next aspect. Don't rush this description, as it will make an impact on those who see it, and you want them to remember it throughout your presentation and afterwards.

Demonstrations are far more difficult to control; indeed, if they can go wrong, they probably will. They can be enormously effective, as everybody likes to see things happening, but you have to realise that part of the attraction, human nature being what it is, lies in waiting to see if something will go wrong and how you will handle the situation if it does. (Calmly, courteously and confidently is the answer to that.) Try to put things right and be willing to ask for help from a member of staff if necessary. They will have had experience of things going wrong and will be sympathetic and helpful, especially if they know that all went well at rehearsal. Sadly, problems can arise within a few minutes: one of us saw an oscillator working perfectly well during a rehearsal, only to see it fail inexplicably half an hour later in front of the audience.

In many cases, there's an answer to such problems. If it's allowed, carry out your demonstration earlier and record it. You can then show it to the audience via the data projector and you can be sure that the audience will see a perfect demonstration, with no problems or hesitations. You are completely in control and can concentrate on giving an effective presentation.

Prototype and demonstration checklist

As you plan your presentation, ask yourself these questions:

- ❏ Is it a good idea to use a prototype?
- ❏ Will the audience be able to see it?
- ❏ Can you use a table or other kind of stand to help them?
- ❏ If so, where will you stand as you talk about your prototype?
- ❏ Do you need a picture of your prototype on the screen?
- ❏ How much time will be taken by showing your prototype to the audience (without speaking)?
- ❏ If you are demonstrating a process to the audience, how can it go wrong?
- ❏ How could you put it right, quickly, in front of the audience?
- ❏ How would you continue your presentation if the demonstration failed completely?
- ❏ Would it be better to record your demonstration and show it through the projector?

● Poster presentations

Nowadays, whatever subject you're studying, you might have to take part in a poster presentation. You will be asked to research and prepare a topic with a poster as your visual aid; yours may be one in a series of posters, each showing a different aspect of the main topic. Your poster will be large, probably A1 size (like a flipchart sheet), but you still have the challenge of producing information so that people who walk round the exhibition, possibly in a group, can see your material clearly, often from as much as a metre away. It's therefore important that your poster should be eye-catching and attractive in layout.

The audience will walk round, looking at each poster in turn, usually before your actual presentation starts. This has the advantage that you can assume some knowledge of what you are talking about before you speak. You may, on the other hand, be asked to make a short presentation, probably only three to five minutes, to each group that has formed in front of your poster, or you may have to answer questions from people as they arrive at your site. Either way, the information in Chapter 2 is relevant. The two biggest potential problems are having too much to say in a short amount of time and having too much information on your poster, so that it looks crowded and unfriendly.

You can't say much, so you need to think through the points that people are most likely to want to know about your work. Draw their attention to, and briefly describe, a couple of aspects which are unusual, new or striking, show where on your poster they can see more and that's about it. Don't try to say too much by speaking quickly, as there's likely to be background noise of other people talking and you won't be heard. Speak slowly and clearly, make eye contact with the person or small group listening and ask if they have any questions when you've said your piece. It's no good embarking on long explanations, as your audience will soon move on; keep your answers brief, but offer to say more if they have time and it seems appropriate.

In preparing your poster, you will need to make an important decision. You might produce an eye-catching design with very little detail so that it does little more than capture the imagination of the audience. This may be useful when you will have time in your presentation to give some of the missing detail. Alternatively, you can produce a very detailed poster which gives the reader a great deal of information and so in your brief presentation you will simply highlight the key features of the poster. Avoid at all costs the temptation to cover all of the information on the poster at breakneck speed. Before you can start to design your poster, you will need to find out about the occasion, the length of time available for the audience to look at the posters, the time available for you to speak, and what the audience is likely to be expecting.

The poster itself mustn't look overcrowded. Several people might look at it at the same time and they won't be able to see small print or tiny details. As far as possible, make your images big and bold and any writing sufficiently large and in a sensible colour (usually blue or black). You probably won't have any very small print and your headings will need to be considerably larger than the text. As with any visual aid, use a normal mixture of upper and lower case bold letters and a simple font such as Arial. It's not a good idea to use text in capital letters, as it's harder to read. Make sure that there's enough blank space, so the text stands out well, and use arrows to direct the reader from one text box to the next. Try to position your most important message in the top half of your poster and as centrally as possible, as that's where people's eyes will rest most naturally. Scan in photographs or other diagrammatic material, again checking that the colours will reproduce clearly without clashing or looking in any way messy. Avoid large chunks of text, which look boring and off-putting.

You might find it helpful to create a mock-up of the poster, using a sheet from a flipchart and sticking text and images to it. Attach it to a wall and then move away and look at it critically. How eye-catching is it? Does it make sense as a whole rather than looking like a collection of unrelated, disparate images? Is the sequence of the material clear? Does an overall message come across at a quick glance?

It's wise to take any opportunity you can get to look at the posters from previous occasions – there are likely to be some available in your department – and see what looks attractive and easy to read, and what doesn't. You will almost certainly be able to get your design made up into a poster and laminated within your own institution, but remember that other students will be doing the same thing, so don't leave it until the last minute. The cost of this varies, and it's worth being aware that academic institutions aren't always the speediest or most cost-effective places to get this work done – large stationery stores with printing facilities can be quicker and cheaper. Make sure that you know how your poster will be attached to the wall or stand, in case you need to take any other equipment with you.

Given the cost of producing and laminating a poster, it's essential that you check every detail; ask several colleagues to check it for you as well. Just one typing error can ruin the whole display, and you won't have a chance for last-minute changes. It would be embarrassing to face an audience while knowing that there's a glaring mistake beside you on your poster.

It's tempting to spend a great deal of time over the poster and very little over what you will say. Prepare your presentation, however short it is, with the same care as you would a full-length PowerPoint presentation. You are likely to be standing beside your poster and so rehearse in this position, deciding as you practise when you might point briefly to a section of the poster itself. This is easier if your design has four or five clearly defined sections. Obviously, your audience can't read all the detail as you point, so you need to make clear exactly what it is you are indicating.

The question-and-answer part of the presentation may, unusually, be longer than the talk itself. Don't ask the audience to read details of the poster as you answer – they won't be able to do so. Try to answer without detailed reference to the poster; if you feel that the details are essential, you might want to produce a handout, perhaps showing the key section from your poster.

Poster presentations can be very helpful to people who have had little experience of giving a full-length presentation. The audience should have seen the poster before you start, and you have an impressive, static visual aid to help them. You yourself, if you are confident in your poster, don't have to worry about handling visual aid equipment as you speak – and the presentation is likely to be short. Good practice!

Poster presentation checklist

You are preparing a poster presentation. Have you:

- ❑ checked previous posters to see what looks attractive and what doesn't?
- ❑ placed your key message where it will be most readily seen, centrally and in the top half of the poster?
- ❑ designed your poster with your key messages in mind, using blank spaces and guiding the reader from one item to the next?
- ❑ chosen a simple font and made the lettering big enough to be read from a metre away?
- ❑ used colour sensibly, especially strong colours like black and blue?
- ❑ checked your poster carefully for errors?
- ❑ allowed plenty of time for your poster to be made up and laminated?
- ❑ checked how your poster will be fixed to its support?
- ❑ used a mock-up of your poster and rehearsed with it so that it feels familiar?

● **Computer demonstrations**

It's becoming more common for students in the sciences, especially computer science and related disciplines, to have to give a computer demonstration. If you have to do this, check exactly what happens in your department, as the details vary. It's likely that you will have to sit at your computer and talk through a piece of work for about ten minutes, while two or three examiners look from over your shoulder or beside you at what you're showing on the screen.

The choices you make in advance about how much you can show will determine whether your demonstration is successful or not. The examiners are interested in what you have produced, whether it's at the right technical depth, is user-friendly, and so on. They need to see these aspects demonstrated, so you need to decide what you can show on the screen as an illustration. Don't be tempted to show a great deal at high speed. The examiners aren't just assessing your work; they're also interested in your introduction to the topic with its overview, how much detail you've chosen to give next, whether it's sensible for such a short presentation, whether they can see clearly and follow a logical progression of information, and the pace at which you're both speaking and using the screen. Computers can show lots of information very rapidly, so you must ensure that you are in control; 'don't rush', always a good maxim in speaking to an audience, is especially important in this type of presentation.

Rehearsal is essential: you need to time your presentation well and make sure that all is ready when the examiners reach you. After you've given your talk, you will probably be asked questions, and of course you'll think about these in advance and make as good a guess as possible about what they will ask. At this point you can make eye contact, which was difficult before, so take the opportunity to look at the examiners and appear friendly and interested in what they have to say. Answer as clearly and concisely as you can.

With any presentation, your success will depend largely on the time you spend preparing not only what you will say but also how you will say it, and what the likely questions will be. Even in a computer demonstration, the essential relationship is between you and your audience, not between the audience and the visual aids; if you use your visuals effectively, they will be a support to you and instrumental in your success, but you must always be in control.

Computer demonstration checklist

You are preparing a computer demonstration. Have you:

- ❑ considered where you will sit and how easy it will be for your audience to see the screen?
- ❑ introduced your topic in a sensible overview?
- ❑ thought carefully about the points which need to be shown on the computer, without unnecessary detail?
- ❑ chosen a reasonable amount of material which can be shown and discussed without being rushed?
- ❑ rehearsed and timed your presentation?

Top Tips

- Have an introductory slide with your name and the subject of your talk on it
- *Never* show irrelevant images or inappropriate cartoons
- Allow at least twenty seconds of silence per image
- Use as little punctuation on the screen as you can get away with
- Avoid blocks of capitals, as they are difficult to read
- Have a simple background with good colour contrast in the image
- Rehearse with all your equipment and material, in the venue if possible
- Avoid fussy movement on the screen or irritating sound effects
- Make sure that everyone can see demonstrations, prototypes, etc.
- On your poster, put the main message centrally towards the top
- Use a mock-up of your poster to check its impact on the audience
- Whatever your visual aids, don't rush them – give the audience time to look

4 Speaking as Part of Your Course

This chapter helps you to

▶ prepare well and take an active part in seminars
▶ read a paper effectively to students and your tutor
▶ make the most of tutorial opportunities
▶ identify your audience and an appropriate style for your talk
▶ use spoken rather than written language
▶ make good notes which will support you as you speak
▶ time your presentation precisely
▶ prepare for a viva and make the most of it

In this chapter, we'll be looking at some of the occasions when you'll find yourself having to prepare and deliver a form of spoken exercise, whether it's formal or informal, assessed or not assessed, by yourself or as part of a group. We'll consider the implications of each situation and how you should approach it, and the type of notes you will need to prepare. Chapter 2 has given you a great deal of advice about how to deliver your presentation, how to use your voice effectively and how to support what you say by appropriate NVC (body language). That advice forms the background to this chapter.

Some of the forms of spoken communication that we'll discuss here won't apply to every course in further or higher education. You'll soon see that if you're reading an arts subject, for instance, you're less likely to make a formal group presentation (although that doesn't mean it couldn't happen). If, on the other hand, you're reading engineering, you will almost certainly have to make formal group presentations but you're unlikely to have to read a seminar paper. Most students never have a viva, but we've included a section about vivas for those who do. So pick and choose the sections of this chapter and the next which are especially relevant to your course, and perhaps skim-read the rest so that you're not taken entirely by surprise if you suddenly find yourself presenting in a form that you didn't expect.

We'll start with seminars, especially seminar papers, and tutorials, and later in the chapter we'll discuss seminar presentations, other formal speaking occasions and vivas. As educational institutions use these terms in different ways, we'll define how we use the words: a seminar is a small class, often a dozen or so people, which meets to hear the introduction to a topic and then discuss it, often informally; a tutorial consists of a meeting between an individual student, or a small number of students, and a tutor, at which a piece of work is analysed and discussed. Tutorials are usually informal, and may include a wider range of subjects for discussion if the participants feel it would be helpful to do so.

● Seminar papers

We've suggested a difference between seminar papers and seminar presentations, although in practice the difference isn't altogether clear. Our distinction is that if you're asked to read a seminar paper, you will have a script in front of you and, for the most part, you'll be reading. You will be assessed on your material and the planning and thinking which have gone into its preparation. Your lecturer may collect a copy of your paper for marking purposes (if you aren't sure, ask whether the written form is to be marked or not). If you make a seminar presentation, the way in which you present your material will be assessed as well as what you say, and the occasion is likely to be more formal. If you're studying a scientific or technical subject, you may have to give a presentation which is very formal and you are likely to be part of a group. We will discuss this type of presentation in Chapter 5. We'll start with the occasions which are likely to be less formal, those involving seminar papers.

The exact form of a seminar paper varies from department to department, but generally it falls into one of three categories: a tutor-led seminar, a student-led seminar and a seminar with a guest speaker. In any of these forms, but especially the second, you're being given an excellent opportunity to learn, try out ideas and assess how your study is going. This may seem to be a large claim, but look at it like this: in a lecture, you might be one of two hundred students sitting in an enormous lecture theatre and removed, physically and possibly emotionally, from what is going on. In a seminar group, there may be only a dozen or so of you sitting together round a table with the lecturer, probably in the lecturer's own room or a special seminar room which might contain the departmental library. You have a far greater opportunity to speak, ask questions or put forward ideas of your own. Seminars are often quite informal and you will be encouraged to join in and listen to other people's ideas and how they are received. If you want to check a detail, there may well be a book immediately available and the seminar may pause while it's checked; if you want to query a point with the lecturer, you can do so there and then.

Tutor-led seminars

In a tutor-led seminar, the topic to be discussed will be introduced by the tutor, although you'll have been given advance warning so that you can read the appropriate text or some background material before the seminar starts. The tutor will speak first and will then open the session to the group so that you can comment or ask questions, and, with luck, there will be an interesting and challenging discussion.

This will happen only if people are well prepared. If you've done the reading, using the guidance you've been given in reading lists, thought about the subject and identified one or two questions to ask, you will be able to participate fully in the seminar. This isn't always easy, though, and you may want to listen on one or two occasions before you actually speak. If everyone does this, it will be a quiet seminar (except for the lecturer), but don't worry too much; most tutors are quite used to having to do much of the talking at first!

You may feel awkward about speaking, in case what you say is 'wrong' or sounds naive or even stupid to other students. Try not to dwell on this too much. An experienced lecturer will make sure that your contribution is taken seriously, and will make an encouraging comment even if your suggestion isn't ideal. The other students will be only too glad that you've spoken and reduced the burden on them!

So, as long as you've carried out the preparation sensibly, listened to what's said and made notes, partly to help you to remember and partly so that you can see what questions will be appropriate, your contribution will be welcome. If you want to ask a question, take a deep breath, relax as far as you can and speak up so that everyone can hear. Don't rush and, if you find that the words aren't coming out quite as you expected, don't be afraid to pause and repeat your question. If you smile and admit that you didn't say it as clearly as you'd intended, everyone will be attentive and sympathetic as you reword the question. You will also feel a great deal better for having spoken; it's waiting to speak for the first time that's most unnerving.

This is one of the good side-effects of speaking at a seminar: each time, it becomes a little bit easier so that by the time you have to lead a seminar, you feel less apprehensive about hearing your own voice.

24-hour checklist

You have to go to a tutor-led seminar in about 24 hours' time. Have you:

- ❏ read the appropriate text or background material? If not, at least make a start now.
- ❏ thought about the subject and your own reaction to it?
- ❏ identified one or two questions that you'd like to ask?

Incidentally, don't feel that the questions have to be challenging, as if you're trying to undermine what has been said. They may simply be requests for more information about a point you found especially interesting or for the repetition of something which wasn't clear. You are unlikely to be assessed in a tutor-led seminar, so you can try out an idea that you might hesitate to put forward in an essay.

Student-led seminar papers

Sometime within your first term, you're likely to be asked to lead a seminar. You will probably be invited to introduce a topic, although it might be reduced to a single aspect of the subject, as you're probably going to have to speak for ten minutes or so. This might seem like forever but is in practice a very short amount of time. The topic will then widen out into a discussion, with the tutor playing a discreet role as required. So essentially you are going to start a discussion and it's a good idea to keep this in mind, as it means that you don't have to answer everything: it's perfectly accept-able for you to say, 'I still haven't made up my mind about this aspect, and I'll be interested in your thoughts on the subject', or something like that.

You will probably be expected to read your paper, and reading to an audience isn't an easy thing to do, although you can make things better for yourself by employing some of the suggestions in the following exercise.

Exercise

- Take half a page of ordinary print, for example in a textbook, and read it aloud. Try to see where the difficulties lie. You will find it hard to look up at your audience, as you'll easily lose your place. You may also find that you tend to speed up, especially in the last two or three lines when the end is in sight.
- Type out the piece of text in one-and-a-half-line spacing rather than single spacing. Use a slightly bigger font.
- Take a highlighter pen and emphasise the key words or phrases that you want to stress.
- Use a different coloured pen to mark pauses (like bar lines in music, vertically across the lines) where you need to make a small break in your speech (for instance to emphasise an important point). Start a new paragraph when you need a longer break (for instance as you move from one aspect of the topic to another). Write 'slow down' in red letters in the margin near the end.
- Now read the passage again and see how much easier it is to put variety into it and occasionally to pause long enough to look at your audience.

By now, you'll have some ideas about the type of script you will use. If you read, it will become monotonous and probably too fast. If you prepare it thoroughly, you can read more effectively, stressing what is important and giving your audience time to think and yourself time to look at them now and then, which in turn will help them to concentrate.

First, though, you must gather your material and decide what you want to say. Don't leave this too late: it will be embarrassing if it's clear to the lecturer and the other students that you haven't really prepared your ideas. You also need to give yourself the opportunity to read it through aloud two or three times to make sure that you can deliver it effectively.

Look for an aspect which is controversial or particularly interesting and use it as the basis of what you're going to say. It's probably safe to assume that some of the group won't be well prepared, so be ready to fill in a bit of background first and then introduce your main point, asking the audience a question if it's appropriate. They can then think about this as you go on talking and should be able to contribute at the end. Give two opposing points of view if your topic is controversial. At this stage, don't try to give references for what you say, although you should have them available in case you're asked.

You will be surprised at how little can be said in ten minutes. Be clear about what you want to say in this limited time. You might choose to leave your audience with a question or a statement which you feel will surprise them or make them want to express a differing opinion – and that's about all you have time for. The discussion will then be opened up, perhaps with a few words from the tutor.

As you are the one who introduced the topic, you are likely to be faced with some questions, at least to begin with. Try to predict before the seminar what your audience might ask and how you would answer. If you get a difficult question, take your time and, if it helps, ask for a moment to think about the question briefly before you give your answer. Remember never to seem harsh to questioners: 'I'm not sure that I've understood your question' is better than 'You're not making it clear'; 'I don't entirely go along with that' is wiser than 'You're wrong'; 'We may have to agree to differ about this' may be safer than 'That's nonsense.' This tact is very important, not just to maintain good relations among the group, but also because you will be part of the audience yourself at the next seminar and you don't want any retaliation!

24-hour checklist

You have to give a seminar paper in about 24 hours' time. Have you:

- ❏ prepared your subject, researching it as far as time and resources permit and deciding what your key point will be?
- ❏ printed out your paper in one-and-a-half-line spacing and marked it up for emphasis and pauses?
- ❏ read it aloud several times so that you're familiar with it (perhaps trying it out on a friend)?
- ❏ thought about the questions that you might be asked afterwards?

If you have done all these things, you are not only likely to give an impressive seminar paper but you will have studied a topic in depth. This will give you confidence in your coursework in general and later may help you in the exams too.

Guest speakers

You may occasionally have the opportunity to go to a seminar taken by a visiting speaker, perhaps someone whose name is well known in your field of study. Such a speaker is likely to have up-to-date research to talk about and he or she will be especially interested in questions, as they will show what people are interested in or maybe disagree with.

It's useful for you to be part of the audience and learn about such an expert's ideas, and there's no reason why you shouldn't ask a question if you want to do so. This isn't easy, as there may be a number of senior members of staff present, as well as other students, and you may understandably be afraid of saying the 'wrong' thing. Take notes as you listen and jot down any question that occurs to you. Listen carefully to make sure that it isn't answered within the talk and that you still think it's a relevant question to ask. Take a deep breath, put a hand up so that the person chairing the session notices you and then speak slowly and clearly. Be careful not to go on too long: a rambling question wastes time and can be irritating to the speaker and the rest of the audience but as long as you word it clearly and briefly, you are likely to impress other people. Smile at the speaker when your question is answered and say thank you. You will rightly feel pleased with yourself for having had the confidence to ask, and the guest will probably be delighted that a student has shown such interest. What's more, it will be much easier for you to speak in public next time.

If you find that you are asked to chair such a session, read the section in Chapter 7 that gives you tips about how to do this effectively (see pp. 124–33).

2-hour checklist

You are going to hear a guest speaker in 2 hours' time. Have you:

- ❑ found out what the subject is and who the speaker is?
- ❑ thought about the subject and whether you have a special interest that you might want to ask about?
- ❑ allowed time to discuss the subject socially afterwards if you have the opportunity?

You will be involved in seminars from time to time, either as part of the audience or as a speaker, and you will also be taking part in tutorials, which are more individual and which we'll look at next.

● Tutorials

Tutorials take place between a tutor and a very small number of students, sometimes just one or two. They are held following the submission of a piece of work such as an essay, giving the tutor the chance to make comments and discuss the work, and the student(s) the chance to ask questions, gain extra information and find out what were the good and less-good features of their work. For these reasons, tutorials are sometimes called supervisions.

In one form of tutorial, you have to take your essay and read it to your tutor and perhaps a fellow student, and they then discuss it with you. If you have to do this, try to read slowly and gauge, as far as you can, how your tutor is reacting to what you read. It would be useful to take a second (and, if appropriate, a third) copy of the essay, so that you can both (all) see it at the same time. Be ready to add notes to your copy as you get comments or queries. More commonly, however, you will have handed the essay in and it will have been returned to you. You then take it along to the tutorial in order to discuss with your tutor (and perhaps a fellow student) both the essay and the mark you were given. There are enormous advantages in this system, which is far more common in higher education in the UK than in the rest of Europe, where classes are commonly much bigger and individual contact is rare. You have the benefit of being able to discuss your work in private and get an informed opinion of it.

In a tutorial, you can:

- talk more or less on a one-to-one basis with your tutor, as opposed to speaking in front of other people
- ask your tutor to repeat something, explain it more fully or fill in background for you, exactly as you want
- listen to your tutor's comments and the additional information you are being given
- make notes for future reference, asking the tutor to wait while you do so
- ask why the tutor felt that the mark was appropriate and, if necessary, what you can do to raise your grades in future
- discuss your own general progress and whether you are on course for your hoped-for results
- ask for clarification of a point you didn't follow in a lecture.

In other words, there are enormous opportunities in a tutorial, as long as you make use of them, but you need to prepare the agenda – after all, it's for your benefit. When you get your essay back from your tutor, read it through and make a note of anything you want to ask about, perhaps using a highlighter pen. Read the tutor's comments carefully and highlight anything you don't understand or can't read. Think about the mark you've been given and decide why it's as good as it is or why it might have been better. If you're not sure, make a note to ask. Don't forget the good aspects: if this seems to be the best essay you've ever written, you can reasonably ask why it was so well received and how you can build on this for future work. It's easy to be depressed by the critical comments and overlook the encouraging ones. Think more generally too: are there questions you'd like to ask about the course, your progress or future issues such as a dissertation? As long as you are courteous and obviously want to know, and are prepared to listen, you will gain a great deal from every tutorial.

Day-before checklist

You have a tutorial tomorrow. Have you:

- ❑ read the essay again and assessed its strengths and weaknesses?
- ❑ marked any passages that you want to ask about?
- ❑ taken note of the lecturer's written comments and highlighted any that you want to discuss?
- ❑ thought about the mark and why it might have been given?
- ❑ assessed the course and how you think you're getting on?
- ❑ thought of any more general questions that you might raise?

● **Presentations**

In the following sections, we've made a rather artificial distinction between seminar presentations and formal presentations. Speaking at a seminar may, as we've seen, involve reading a paper; it may also be the occasion for you to make a presentation which may be more or less formal, involving visual aids and a question and answer session at the end. Especially if you're studying a scientific or technical subject, you may also be asked to give a very formal presentation, probably as part of a group, in which your department tries hard to produce the sort of setting and response that you might meet in industry if, for example, you were speaking to a group of your company's clients.

It's worth saying that the presentation you may be asked to give as part of a job interview is likely to be of the latter sort: very formal, strictly timed and with a question and answer session at the end.

Seminar presentations

You may be asked to give a seminar presentation either individually or as one of a pair of students or, depending on your subject, as a group. In either case, you will be marked not only on your subject matter but also on the way in which you deliver your talk, principally the way in which you create a rapport with the audience, your voice and your body language. (These aspects were discussed in Chapter 2.) In this chapter, we'll consider how to prepare for these events, especially the notes from which you'll be speaking. You may be expected to use visual aids, and you may be part of a group, but again we discuss these aspects separately (Chapters 3 and 5 respectively).

Please don't think, 'The subject I'm studying is one that involves essays and seminar papers, so I can skip the rest of this chapter.' Sooner or later, a formal presentation may catch up with you, as many departments which in the past didn't think that this form of communication was relevant to their subject are now using it as an assessed part of the course. What's more, an increasing number of employers now expect a formal presentation as part of the interview procedure for new recruits, and a job interview isn't the best occasion on which to make your first presentation.

In a seminar presentation, you may be asked to prepare an introduction to a topic or put forward a point of view. In the latter situation, one of your colleagues may be giving the opposite case. You may prepare your own material without reference to your partner, but it's as well to think together about questions and which aspects of your material are most likely to be controversial. In this kind of presentation (and indeed in all kinds) you must remain calm and rational. However strongly you feel about the subject, it's the arguments that matter and they must be delivered in a controlled and courteous way, although not necessarily without personal feeling. However much you dislike the points put forward by the other speaker, you have to treat them seriously and thoughtfully, and recognise that people may feel just as strongly on the other side.

In making this type of presentation, you may have to speak for 15–20 minutes and you will be using notes rather than a full script. This might sound daunting, but it's actually a bonus from your point of view, as we'll show later. It's unlikely that anyone will interrupt your talk unless you say something which is factually wrong, and, even if you do, the lecturer may wait until the end before telling you (and the group). There will probably be a question and answer session when you've finished.

You'll notice that we've tended to say 'may' and 'probably', as there are many different requirements of a seminar presentation and you need to clarify what is expected of yours.

You may also want to ask the questions that we discuss below, as they could be helpful, whatever form of presentation you're making.

Formal presentations

The first stage of your preparation for a formal presentation is to find out as much as you can about your audience and about what will be expected of you. Ask the lecturer concerned the following questions:

- Who will be in the audience and approximately how many will there be?
- How long will you have to speak for?
- When should questions be asked?
- Are you expected to use visual aids?
- What is being assessed, and does any material have to be handed in for marking?

You may be a bit surprised by the first question, but it's worth asking. If your audience consists of your lecturer and your fellow students, the level which you choose for your material and at which questions are likely to be asked is clearly going to be your own level, that of the students in the class. However, if staff or research students are going to be invited, you may feel that you need to carry out more research and be prepared for questions that probe your understanding rather more deeply. Nobody is likely to ask unfair questions, but staff don't always appreciate the level of student understanding, especially in a technical subject, and you have to be ready to say that you don't know and not lose confidence as you say it. It's possible that someone might ask a question even though they think that you probably won't know the answer, just so they can make everyone think about the issue, perhaps before developing it in a subsequent lecture.

It's also wise to get used to finding out who will be in your audience. As you prepare a presentation for a job interview, you will need to think carefully about what your audience will want to hear (see Chapter 8), and when you are at work, the knowledge and experience of your audience will be critically important in determining the way in which you approach a presentation. You will also want to know roughly how many people will be in the audience, not least so that if you want to make a handout (see pp. 53–5), you know how many copies will be needed. If you have a small number in the audience, it might be acceptable to sit down while you speak, but if there are more than a dozen or so, you will need to stand. Your visual aids will be affected, too: if you are speaking to a few people, you won't need to project very far, and you might be able to use a flipchart or smaller print in your visual aids than if you have a large audience (see p. 38–9). It's rare to know exactly how many people will come, but well worth finding out approximately how many there might be.

Be clear about the length of your talk. Does your time limit include the question and answer session or is it additional? You will need to rehearse to make sure that you're within the limit, allowing a little extra time for unavoidable interruptions or delays (see also p. 80). It's difficult to get the timing right if people interrupt, so, if the structure of the presentation allows, ask for questions and comments at the end. If you've been given twenty minutes including questions, decide how much time you want to allow for discussion, perhaps five or even ten minutes at the end of your presentation. It's much more likely, though, that you'll have extra time at the end of your talk for the audience to ask questions. They need to be told. If members of your audience aren't sure when they are allowed to ask questions, they will worry about this problem rather than listening to you. An important part of your introduction, therefore, is to let them know when questions are appropriate. If you tell them, they're unlikely to inter-rupt your talk.

Visual aids are generally considered to be an essential part of a formal presentation but a very short seminar presentation might take place without visual material. It would still be wise to check with the tutor that you haven't misunderstood the requirements. If you have a choice, remember that visual aids are a support for the speaker as well as the audience. You will probably know what type of equipment is available (and expected): in a seminar presen-tation, the OHP is still quite common, although for a formal presentation, as you know from Chapter 3, you may well be using a data projector or a smartboard.

You will be assessed on the material you present, and you may also be assessed on your presentation technique and style and on your visual aids. You may have to hand in your notes as part of the assessment, in which case they probably need to be written out again more fully than when you used them. Find out exactly what is being assessed and roughly how much weight is being given to different aspects: lecturers sometimes give sepa-rate marks for the way in which you use your voice (see pp. 6–18), your NVC (see pp. 21–30), your teamwork if you are part of a group, and so on. Knowing which points score marks helps you to concentrate on key aspects in rehearsal. Should you produce printouts of your visual material as part of the assignment or extra copies of handouts? Again, you can have your material ready if you know it's going to be collected and marked.

Assessment checklist

Which of the following are being assessed in your presentation?

- ❑ Your material, its accuracy and structure
- ❑ If you are in a group, your teamwork
- ❑ Your notes and how you use them
- ❑ The way in which you use your voice, its clarity, pace and emphasis
- ❑ Your NVC
- ❑ The rapport you build with the audience
- ❑ Your visual aids and how you use them
- ❑ How well you keep to time
- ❑ How you handle questions

Many of these topics are discussed in other chapters, but now we're particularly interested in the form of notes you make and the most effective ways of using them.

Making and using notes

Notes are important in a presentation to help you to remember what you want to say. This seems obvious, but we'd like to stress *help you to remember*. The purpose of notes isn't to tell you what to say – you need to know that already and to be ready to practise until you are familiar and at ease with all that you want to communicate. However, nerves can have odd effects on your performance and under the stress of giving a presentation you might forget what you'd prepared, and notes are then props to support you. It isn't just what you want to say, it's the order in which you want to make your points. You might accidentally introduce something in the wrong place, so that the audience isn't prepared for it and can't understand it, or, of course, you might simply leave out a key point and remember it only when it's become irrelevant.

There's yet another danger in speaking without notes, which is not always considered. You might say more than you intended to. Because you're free from the constraints of notes, you could more easily be sidetracked and give information which you're not sure about, statistics which haven't been checked, or, worst of all, you might reveal something which is confidential. Notes help to keep you on track.

We're not saying that you should never speak without notes. As you become more experienced and more confident, you may decide that some sections of your presentation could be managed without the need for a prompt. Eventually, you might feel that you could give the whole talk in this way, and you could be right. However, you might be wrong, and standing in front of a large number of influential people isn't the best time to find out.

Dangerous notes Let's start by discussing the forms of notes which we don't recommend. It's never a good idea to use A4 paper for your notes, as it's big enough to be obvious to the audience and you can just about hide your face behind it, thus preventing any of the audience from lip-reading. Look again at the cartoon figure on page 8. If you're nervous, a large sheet of paper is surprisingly noisy. If your hands shake, it rattles.

The most serious problem with A4 paper, however, is that it tempts you to write out the whole script, word for word, which you then read to the audience. Earlier in this chapter, we showed how to prepare a script if you *have* to read it, but we warned how hard it is to read aloud effectively. Don't put yourself in this position for a formal presentation: you will be expected to use notes; a full script will only cause additional difficulties for you.

One of these problems is the different registers of language that we use in writing and speaking. If we're writing a formal document, such as a dissertation or report, we will be writing impersonally, frequently using the passive ('It was found that . . .', rather than 'I found . . .'), and we'll tend to choose formal words (we might describe an unfortunate visual aid as 'over-complicated' when in speech we'd probably use 'fussy'). We have to give emphasis by the way in which we choose and order our words and sentences, and occasionally by using italics, as we did with the word 'have' in the previous paragraph. If this is of particular interest to you, you might like to look at two of our other books, *Effective Communication for Arts and Humanities Students* and *Effective Communication for Science and Technology* (see Further Reading), in which we discuss in detail the qualities of good writing. This formality in writing comes largely from the fact that we are removed from our readers. We don't know, for instance, who you, our present reader, is, or much about you. You might pass your copy of this book on to someone in a different country in several years' time, and we wouldn't know. We've deliberately chosen to write in a comparatively informal style, part way between writing and speaking, in order to sound friendly and accessible; if we were writing a report or dissertation, we would write in a much less personal way.

In speaking, we have our audience right there in front of us. We know quite a lot about them, how many there are, what they want to know and that they're listening (we hope) now, as we speak. We therefore want to build a rapport with them, share our experience and discuss our ideas with them. We say 'I' and 'you' frequently, we use friendly words that make an immediate impact ('big' rather than 'substantial'), we repeat our key points in case they were missed the first time and we give emphasis by the way in which we use our voices and gestures (see Chapter 2). Our audience will soon start to fall asleep if we don't involve them and talk directly to them. We can't do this if we're reading a full script. We need to look at the audience and gauge their response, and we need to sound as if we really are talking to them: that is, using spoken rather than written language. Occasionally, speakers try to learn their script by heart, rather as an actor learns his or her lines. Acting and speaking to an audience obviously have much in common, but there are also important differences. An actor rarely speaks directly to the audience: they 'overhear' the actor talking to other people on stage, and it's these other people with whom the actor is building a relationship. This is transmitted to those who are watching. If the lines of the play are changed, other actors will know and may be unnerved, while in a presentation the words will change slightly each time you speak them and it won't matter. If the actor forgets the lines, there's also usually someone prompting in the wings. You don't have that luxury when you make a presentation! These differences mean that you aren't in a play and shouldn't think of learning your lines.

So, what are the most effective and professional forms of notes to use?

Good notes: file cards If you find that you can give your presentation entirely from visual aid prompts on the screen (see below), and if you rehearse sufficiently, you will find that they are useful as a form of notes, although limited in their content in a way that note cards aren't. This is why many experienced and professional speakers regularly use small file cards, which are good to hold and give support at every stage of a talk. We recommend their use whenever you're speaking from notes rather than a full script: they don't rustle or flop around as A4 paper does; you can't easily hide behind them; because they are unobtrusive your audience will hardly notice that you're using them. As you finish with each card, slip it to the back of the pile in your hand. Don't fasten the cards together, as this makes it harder to handle them, but do number them just in case they get out of order.

How much you choose to write on each card will depend partly on your familiarity with the subject and partly on your nerves, but we'd suggest that you write on every other line and leave a margin for additional comments (see below). Try to make your writing slightly larger than usual and, of course, make sure that it's clear and legible. If you crowd your cards with detailed information, you will have to study them at length instead of seeing their contents at a glance. It's a good idea to highlight a few key words on each card using a coloured pen, so that you can see them quickly and easily.

You might want to write out the first sentence or two of your talk in full, to reassure yourself that you will have no difficulty in beginning. After that, write out only key words and phrases. Remember the problem of using the wrong register of language: if you write your notes in full, they will sound as if they were meant for a book rather than a presentation; if you write just the key words, you'll form them into sentences as you speak and they will be in spoken language. However, some information always needs to be written out, such as figures that you might forget or quotations from someone else's text. It would be embarrassing if, for instance, you forgot the price of the product you were discussing. Write it on your cards and it will be there in case you hesitate.

Cards which have a small amount of information on them, which are clearly written in fairly large lettering and on which the two or three most important words are highlighted are easy to use. You can glance at them from time to time as you speak or look at them for longer while the audience is studying a new visual aid. They will reassure you that you're giving the right material in the right order. Any statistics you need to include will be recorded so you can refer to them if necessary and, above all, your nerves will be steadied by the knowledge that you have good notes to support you and that the audience will scarcely notice that you have notes at all.

As an example, let's look at a note card written by a student studying art history. She is giving a short presentation on stained glass, with particular reference to Wells Cathedral.

This is one of her first attempts at notes:

The east window as you can see from the slide is sometimes called the Golden Window, as there's yellow glass round the borders, for the inscriptions and the crowns. The colours of mediaeval glass were produced by adding different metallic oxides to the crucibles that held the molten glass. Cobalt gave blue, copper gave green, manganese gave purple and iron gave red. In the fourteenth century they discovered that white glass could be stained yellow by using silver sulphide, with the results that can be seen here. Stained glass appears to be its own light source and so it's at its best on a dull day.

This is more or less what the student wrote in her essay; she hasn't really made the transition from a written to a spoken style. You will find how difficult it is to read aloud if you try. Part of the problem is that, apart from 'you' near the start, there's nothing personal about the style – it doesn't relate to the audience. There's also a longish list in the middle. She has a slide on the screen, and so some of what is being said can be seen by speaker and audience alike, but the speaker seems unaware of that.

It might be helpful to look next at what the speaker might *say* in giving this information.

> You can see from the slide why this is called the Golden Window – look at all that yellow glass round the borders and in the crowns. It was as late as the fourteenth century that they learnt how to make yellow glass – they stained white glass yellow by using silver sulphide. How did they get all those other colours? Well, while the glass was still molten, they added different metallic oxides to the crucibles. You can see they managed realistic pinks for the skin colours and those splendid greens and blues for robes and suchlike – in case you're wondering, they used copper for the green and cobalt for the blue. They're wonderfully rich colours, aren't they? You can see how stained glass seems to be its own light source – it's best if we look at it on a dull day – so we're lucky, aren't we?

Most of the information is the same – although, wisely, the list has been short-ened – but the style is different. The first word is 'you' to attract the audience – they are asked to look for themselves; 'we' makes them feel that they and the speaker are sharing the experience, and the speaker isn't afraid to introduce a personal note in 'splendid' and 'wonderfully rich'. The audience is asked a question in the middle that they don't have to answer, and they are left at the end with a touch of humour and a question that invites their agreement.

Now this has to be turned into a note card to speak from, assuming that the speaker knows what she wants to say, has rehearsed, and needs only prompts or reminders.

> Slide = east window - Golden Window, look at yellows.
> C14, stained white glass with silver sulphide to produce that yellow
> Other colours - adding metallic oxides to molten glass in crucibles –
> copper – green, cobalt – blue
> Point out greens and blues for robes, and the realistic pink for flesh
> Stained glass own light source – best on dull day

You'll notice that the critical words that could easily be forgotten – 'metallic oxides', 'copper – green, cobalt – blue' are written out, while words that are easy to remember, such as the yellow borders and crowns that they are all looking at, can be left to the speaker's memory. This will be much easier to speak from than a fully written text.

Earlier, we suggested that you draw a margin on your cards in which you can write messages for yourself. It's a good idea to record when you want to show each visual aid, using perhaps just a coloured asterisk in the margin at the appropriate point on the card. Nerves can make you speed up and encourage you to move the slide on too quickly, before the audience has had time to study the information. On the other hand, you might forget to show a slide and then remember it when it's no longer relevant. A mark on your cards will ensure that you show each slide at the best possible time, just as you rehearsed it.

In the same way, you can make a note of a handout you want to give the audience, either before you start or at the end. If you have to introduce other speakers, make a note of their names in the margin of your card, so that you don't forget under the pressure of the presentation. Many speakers tend to speak quickly but if you write 'slow down' in red letters at the top of each card, you will have constant reminders to watch your speed. If you tend to run your ideas together instead of 'paragraphing' them (see pp. 19, 96), write 'pause' on each card. If you think that nerves might make you look agitated, add 'smile' to your notes as a reminder.

In all these ways, cards can give you more help than any other form of notes, but perhaps their greatest value lies in the fact that they can make sure you time your presentation accurately. This is so important that we will discuss in detail the whole problem of getting the timing right, and why it's so critical to the success or failure of the occasion. First, however, there's another form of notes that needs comment.

Good notes: visual aids   You will probably be using visual aids, which act as reminders both to the audience and to you, the speaker. You may, for instance, have a list of bullet points on the screen which show the content of your talk and the order in which you will be giving it. The audience reads it and, as you look at it, you are reminded of the main points you want to make. The limitation of this form of notes is that as you move on, the list disappears and with it your introductory notes, but you are likely to have other 'notes' to help you as you proceed. You may use each bullet point as the heading of a slide, with more bullet points or illustrations underneath it. You may have to talk through a diagram, and the picture on the screen presents you with your notes: that is, the diagram itself acts as a reminder while you are talking through it. If you use a 'summary' slide at the end, you will again be helped to remember the points you need to make as you conclude.

There are two potential problems with such notes. One is that you will be tempted to write too much on the screen, as a help to you rather than a good visual aid for the people in front of you. You must be able to talk from the limited number of words that it's sensible to put on a slide. Refer back to the example of the visual aid about Cluny on p. 40 to see how this works in practice.

The other problem is that if you need to look at the screen a great deal during your presentation, you will start to make life easier for yourself by gradually turning towards it. In the end, without realising it, you may be giving your presentation to the screen rather than to the audience; you may even be turning your back on some of them.

However, if you are aware of these potential difficulties, you can make sure as you design your slides that you don't have too many words on the screen, and you can ask your colleagues at the rehearsal stage to let you know if you tend to look at the screen too often or for too long. It's a question of setting up the good habit of always looking at and talking to your audience. Once you do that, you are unlikely to turn away from them as you speak.

Both note cards and visual aids can act as practical and efficient forms of notes but, whichever you decide to use, it's essential to practise with them so that you're sure about the overall timing of the talk.

Timing the presentation

We need to say at once that there may be occasions when the time taken by your talk isn't considered to be very important. Seminar papers read to the audience tend to be in this category, and there may be other occasions on which a lecturer will give you such a vague guideline ('You can talk for about twenty minutes, or longer if you have a lot to say') that you know you're not going to be assessed on how accurate your timing is.

On the other hand, any kind of formal presentation tends to have a strict time limit. This is especially true for one of the most important presentations you will ever give, the one that is part of your job interview. Of course, not all such interviews include a presentation, but scientific and technical jobs almost always require candidates to give a short talk, and arts and humanities graduates are increasingly having to follow suit. We'll look at the whole business of interviews in Chapter 8, but the presentation timing will be critical for you at that stage, and it's helpful to have practised accurate timing on previous occasions.

Good timing is important, partly as a matter of courtesy to your audience. People find it difficult to concentrate on a speaker for very long, and they are usually anxious to know when they can relax and ask questions or go for coffee. If you say that you'll speak for 20 minutes and are still in full flow after half an hour, they will feel cheated and irritated, and will tend to remember your bad timing rather than what you said. They also want time to ask questions, and if your talk overruns, there may be only a limited opportunity to do so.

Just as important is the example of your management skills that you're giving to your audience and, in the case of an interview, to potential employers. If you've been given the resources of time, a room, an audience and some equipment, you need to show that you can use them well. If you talk for longer than the time allowed, you're giving the impression that you don't take other people's resources seriously, which could be very damaging if, for instance, you have applied for a job in management.

Preparation is the key to good timing. Very few people can time a talk accurately by instinct, and it's very difficult to adapt your timing as you're actually speaking. As you plan what you will say, keep the time constraint in mind and rehearse until you take slightly less time than your limit. This is important, as the golden principle of timing is:

> *It always takes longer than you think and so leave yourself a bit of time in hand.*

Why does this happen? You have your material planned, you go through it, speaking aloud, and you time the result. You have measured your speaking time, but when you're in front of an audience, there will be extra pauses, for example as you make a strong point and pause for effect or say something witty that makes your audience laugh. There will be activity as you move back to indicate something on the screen or when you sit down while a colleague moves into position to speak. You need to wait in silence to allow your audience time to read and understand your visual material before you begin to speak again. If people arrive late, you pause while they find seats and settle down. All these and similar events take time, but it's almost impossible to assess how long the pauses last until you're actually in front of your audience. This is why, if you're given 20 minutes, it's wise to think in terms of 15 minutes; you'll probably find that you take 18 in the presentation itself.

On the first occasion that you rehearse your talk, you will almost certainly find that you've taken half an hour instead of the 20 minutes you've been allowed. Cut your material until you think that you'll take less than 20 minutes and then try it again. You're likely to find that it's still a bit too long and so you'll need to cut your material again. As soon as you find that you are speaking for 15 minutes, you've got it right. Rewrite your cards to reflect your shortened material and then rehearse again, to make sure!

If you're using file cards, you can add timing messages to help you. Have a card that just says, in red letters, 'Halfway through'. Put this card in the middle of your notes so that when you get to it, you can do a quick time check to see that you are about halfway through the time. Write one or two cards towards the end of your talk in a different colour. These are optional cards: if you have plenty of time, you can include them; if you're short of time, you can leave them out. It's nearly impossible to work out, as you speak to your audience, what you could sensibly miss out if you find you're running short of time. In the case of a group presentation, it's especially important for the last speaker to prepare in this way, as he or she is dependent on other people keeping to time. They should do, but you can never be sure!

There's one other way in which you can use your cards for help with timing. Just before you start, make a quick note of the time you have to finish. This might seem obvious: you are due to begin at 11 a.m., you're allowed 20 minutes, so you finish at 11.20. However, if the previous speaker overruns and you start at 11.12, the timing isn't so clear. If you look at the clock and see 11.20 and realise that you've still some way to go but you don't know when you should stop, you are likely to feel panic, which is never good for a speaker. If you check the time just before you begin, you will know exactly how much time is left, which will increase your confidence.

You may find that, after several rehearsals, you're beginning to ignore your cards because you're no longer dependent on them. This is fine, but we'd recommend that you keep them with you, in case you need them when it comes to the presentation itself. If you then look at them and realise that you're several cards away from what you're actually saying, don't worry. Pause while you find the right card and then continue – the audience will never notice and you will have the prompt you need, right there in your hand.

Note cards checklist

You have written cards to act as notes for your presentation. Ask yourself the following questions:

- ❑ Are my cards clearly written and easy to read?
- ❑ Have I left plenty of space and a margin on each card?
- ❑ Are my cards numbered?
- ❑ Have I written key words and phrases, not sentences?
- ❑ Have I used a highlighter pen on the most important words?
- ❑ Is all the statistical information on the cards so that I won't forget it?
- ❑ Is each change of visual material indicated in the margin?
- ❑ Are handouts shown so that I will remember when to give them out?
- ❑ Have I made notes on my cards about slowing down and pausing?
- ❑ Is there a 'halfway through' card, and are there optional cards towards the end?
- ❑ Have I rehearsed with my notes until I feel at ease with them?

● Vivas

Most students will never have to face a viva, and that's partly why it has such a fearsome reputation: a viva is often seen as some kind of punishment. It isn't. Some courses include a viva for all students automatically, but in most cases it happens because someone wants to discuss your work in order to help you. This may be for any of the following reasons:

- ● You're on the borderline between two grades or classes of degree and the examiners want to give you another chance to get the higher grade or class. Your result will never be lowered as a result of the viva.
- ● Your grades show a wide variation for no apparent reason. You might be asked questions about the topic for which you got the low grade in order to see whether it can be raised to be more in keeping with the rest of your results.
- ● You have a particular problem, such as dyslexia, which might mean that your written work isn't truly representative of your abilities. The viva gives you a chance to shine orally.
- ● Your examiners are being assessed! Occasionally, vivas are held to make sure that your examiners are in line with the overall standard. You can only gain from such a viva.
- ● Your examiners are so impressed that they want to talk to you about the possibility of further work or research.

There's one more reason for a viva, which is an unpleasant one, and that's if there is some suspicion of plagiarism and your examiners want to make sure that you are as knowledgeable as your results suggest. The most common reason for this is if a dissertation or final report contains material which seems to have been taken from another source without being acknowledged. You have to prove that you were the originator of the information and someone else used the same words without your knowledge, and a genuine mistake was made. It isn't easy to prove, so it's worth taking enormous care to make sure that you never end up in this situation.

As you can see, most of the reasons for holding vivas are student-friendly and you can only gain from a viva if you have one. However, you do need to turn up and it's important to keep a look-out for dates and times when you've completed your exams. If you are told that you will be having a viva, you can expect about three examiners to be present, probably including your tutor and an external examiner. In the case of a subject with industrial links, such as engineering, you might have one examiner from a local company which has a good relationship with your department. In any case, there is likely to be at least one person whom you don't know, so it's wise to look reasonably smart and alert so that the first impression they get is a good one.

If you're given sufficient notice, read through your dissertation or final report again before the viva, and perhaps also your recent notes on any aspect of the subject in which you suspect you didn't do well in the exam. If it's appropriate for your area of study, think about any particular difficulties involved in the work or any practical applications it might have. Think about what you've enjoyed most in your course, and any further work that has suggested itself to you.

A viva is a bit like a job interview (see Chapter 8) and you should employ some of the same techniques. Don't worry too much about being nervous: the examiners will expect you to be a bit shaky. Smile at them as you greet them, be ready to shake hands if they offer to do so, sit down only when you're asked to, make eye contact as you answer their questions and don't rush your answers. If it will help you, say 'I need a minute to think about that, please' before you respond. It's much better to give a considered reply than to start too quickly and then become confused, or say something that you regret. Stress can make you irritable or discourteous, and taking your time is a good way of preventing this. When the session is over, smile and thank the examiners – after all, you can only gain from having had the opportunity of a viva.

Viva checklist

You have been told that you have a viva in two days' time. Put the following plan into action:

- ❑ Reread your dissertation or final report.
- ❑ Look at your notes for any aspects of the exams that you found difficult and, if possible, talk to a colleague about them.
- ❑ See the lecturer if there's any material which you don't understand and suspect that you might be asked about.
- ❑ If it's appropriate, think about the practical applications of your work or any possible future developments that you would be interested in.
- ❑ Don't lose sleep over your viva: it's for your benefit.
- ❑ Remember when you go for the viva to try to breathe deeply and relax, be as calm and courteous as possible and see the occasion not as a penalty but as an opportunity.

Top Tips

- Always do the preparatory reading for a seminar and listen before you speak
- Plan questions you might ask or be asked
- Be tactful and mutually supportive
- Make notes at seminars and tutorials
- Prepare in advance useful questions for your tutor at a tutorial
- Find out the basis of the assessment of a presentation
- Use notes – key words not sentences
- Be calm and rational, no matter how strongly you feel
- Be prepared to say that you don't know the answer
- Don't overrun your time limit
- Plagiarism is theft – give the source of your information
- See a viva not as a penalty but as a golden opportunity to improve your result

5 Speaking as Part of a Group

This chapter helps you to:

- ▶ form a presentation group and organise its work
- ▶ practise teamwork, with shared responsibilities
- ▶ choose your subject and limit its scope
- ▶ plan your group image and your venue
- ▶ structure your material and rehearse it
- ▶ handle questions effectively

In previous chapters, we've discussed the various stages of making a presentation, from gathering and organising the material through preparing notes and visual aids to handling your nerves and your NVC when speaking to your audience. Throughout, it's been assumed that you are the only speaker. When you leave education and start work, you'll probably realise very quickly that this isn't necessarily the case. In many areas of employment, you are more likely to be part of a team; if you are asked to make a presentation, you may well be sharing it with several colleagues.

Within your college or university, the form of your presentation will depend to a certain extent on your subject area. On the whole, if you're studying an arts subject, you're less likely to be involved in a group presentation (although as we're including a pair of speakers as a 'group', you may still need some of the advice we're giving). If you are studying a subject such as management, you are almost certainly going to work in a group, and such a presentation is an integral part of most scientific and technical courses.

● Forming a group

If there are only two of you sharing a presentation, you will probably have joined forces because of a common interest in the subject, or because the lecturer has suggested that you share a topic. The advice we'll give later about sharing the workload and rehearsing together will still be useful to you, although if you are simply taking different points of view or dividing the subject in half, it's less important that you work together in the early stages. For instance, if you are both studying archaeology, one of you might give the background to the discovery of a particular site, while the other describes the artefacts found there. It's still essential that you coordinate the research and go through the presentation together, but the material you use doesn't overlap as it might do if, for instance, you were management students discussing the marketing strategy of a local company.

Two problems are common in the formation of groups, whatever their size. If there are several mature students in the class, they may choose to work together, when it would be more useful for them to be divided between several groups. Experienced speakers, especially if they have worked in industry for some years, are valuable to the class, as they appreciate the implications of group work and can often raise the general standard. Spreading this expertise is often better than grouping such people together.

The other potential difficulty arises if there are a number of overseas students in the class who all speak the same language. They are likely automatically to group themselves together, sometimes with the express intention of working in their own language. If this is allowed to happen, their English is unlikely to improve and the lecturer will find it difficult to help them; much assistance is given because the lecturer has overheard a comment or looked over a student's shoulder and noticed a problem. If the language used for discussion and note-making isn't known to the member of staff, this is impossible. Other groups can benefit from the different experience and approach that an overseas student can bring to the topic. The fact that the student has an accent shouldn't be a problem, especially if the other members of the group give help and support as required.

There's no ideal size for a presentation group. Two people can work well together and the potential problem of coordinating the work is minimised. If there are more than four in the group, the presentation must allow them all to have the experience of speaking, which takes quite a long time, probably at least twenty minutes. It may be much harder for the group to get together for preparation and rehearsal out of class time, and someone needs to take the role of coordinator, having everyone's telephone number and email address, reminding them of agreed dates and times and making sure that everyone knows about any decisions that have been made.

Advantages and disadvantages of working as a group

In spite of the difficulties, there are advantages in speaking as part of a pair or a group rather than as an individual:

- The workload and the stress are shared
- You can use a range of abilities
- Variety is built into the occasion, as the audience has different voices to listen to
- You can show how good you are at teamwork.

Let's look at each of these in turn. They are particularly important points, as they apply not only to presentations but also to any work that you approach as a team.

Sharing the burden is a great advantage, as long as everyone takes his or her role seriously. If one person in the group doesn't come to meetings, misses classes and generally opts out of the work, this will rightly be resented by everybody else. If the group can solve this problem by itself, it should do so, but there might come a point at which it's sensible to involve the lecturer, especially if the group is being given a single mark that everyone shares. Most lecturers will have had experience of such a difficulty and will notice that it's happening before the group says anything about it. The opposite problem is equally disruptive: one member of the group can try to dominate, insisting on his or her point of view and wanting to take the largest share of the presentation time. The rest of the group must try to curb this tendency early on, finding out and stressing other people's skills and insisting on a sensible discussion before decisions are made. The lecturer can be brought in if necessary, and again the chances are that the difficulty will have been noticed.

The pair or group who are speaking will need to organise meetings and eventually rehearsals together, and it's essential that everyone takes part. Issues such as the timing of the presentation (see pp. 79–81) are impossible to resolve if someone is missing, and it's important that everybody knows what each member of the team is saying, not least to ensure that they all agree with one another!

Group support Having said this, you should be happy to take part in a group presentation because it allows so much cooperation and mutual support. An instance comes to mind. One of us was teaching a class in which there was a student with serious problems about speaking to an audience – way beyond normal nerves. She was part of a group, but everybody had to speak because the occasion was assessed as part of their coursework. The other students decided they would help and support her, so they organised practice occasions when she simply sat at the front with the others but didn't speak. Then she was encouraged to sit at the front and answer a question. Still sitting down, she was helped to introduce another speaker. At every stage, the other students congratulated her and encouraged her to continue. When it came to the group presentation, she actually managed to stand at the front and give a brief introduction. At the end, both staff and students went out of their way to let her know how well she'd done. The problem didn't go away and she may never become an enthusiastic speaker, but she had coped with it because of the support of her group. She would certainly never have succeeded if she had been asked to make an individual presentation.

Even if your group is a random selection of individuals, it's likely to include different abilities. If there are only two of you, one will probably have a stronger voice than the other (think about using the strong voice to begin and end your presentation, with the softer voice in the middle) or perhaps one has more experience of designing visual aids than the other. In a larger group, you may have a natural leader who will encourage the group and help to keep it united. As long as this person doesn't try to dominate, having him or her to take a lead is useful. If one student takes responsibility for the visual aids, make sure there's a back-up copy that is easily available, as it could be this student who gets flu at the last moment and is confined to bed. It will be expected that the presentation will go ahead as planned in spite of this setback and the visual aids will be essential.

At one of your earliest meetings, encourage everyone to put forward ideas or volunteer their own expertise. This isn't easy: many gifted people are shy and afraid of seeming to boast about their talents, and you may need someone who is good at asking questions and encouraging a response (a most valuable member of the team!) to assess what the group members have to offer.

Try to ensure that the work is distributed in a fair way. If there is interviewing to be done, allocate more than one person to this so that they can go together, which will give them confidence. If you are likely to use a prototype, suggest that two or three people are involved in producing it. Visual aids may be the preserve of one person, but see that someone else discusses their content and checks it afterwards.

New team checklist

You are part of a newly formed team, preparing a presentation. Have you:

- ❏ introduced yourselves so that you all know each other?
- ❏ exchanged email addresses and telephone numbers?
- ❏ found out what work/speaking experience group members have?
- ❏ discussed possible topics to check strong likes/dislikes?
- ❏ chosen a coordinator for meetings?
- ❏ listened carefully to one another to gauge interests and abilities?
- ❏ ensured that everyone will take their fair share of the workload?

When it comes to allocating roles in the presentation itself, assuming that all group members have to speak, look first at your topic and decide how to divide it into sections. Never use the 'three speakers for fifteen minutes, therefore five minutes each' approach: if you do, you will overrun (see p. 80), and it's unlikely that the topic will divide itself so neatly. The exception to this is a talk based on two people giving both sides of the question. If two philosophy students are asked to give a talk on euthanasia, one for and one against, they will divide the time more or less equally between them, or the audience will feel that they aren't getting a fair picture of the issue. More commonly, it's the subject itself that matters: some aspects, such as the technical content of an engineering presentation, will inevitably take longer than the cost implications of the product described. Divide the time allocated into the different aspects that need to be included and then discuss who should take each role. Sometimes this is obvious, sometimes not. On the whole, you should use a strong speaker to start and perhaps sum up, and maybe give a briefer section to the weakest or most reluctant speaker. Don't assume that the shyest and quietest person in the group is a poor speaker. Surprisingly, such people may come to life in front of an audience, while the loudest and perhaps most assertive person may crumble in the same situation.

Variety is important in a presentation, especially a long one (more than about twenty minutes). We wrote earlier about the need to change pace and volume (pp. 6–13) and the need for visual aids to help to keep the audience's attention (pp. 34–5). A change of speaker can be just as useful: a different personality and a different voice increases the audience's concentration briefly. You can use this to emphasise a particularly important fact by including it just after the new speaker has started – not right at the beginning, as the audience needs a few seconds to adjust, but early on in what he or she is saying.

Teamwork is of paramount importance in many jobs and taking part in a group presentation may give you your first experience of working in this way. It's more important for the future than students often realise: when you go for a job interview (see Chapter 8), you may be asked whether you've worked as part of a team and how you felt about it. Having taken part in a group presentation means that you have experience to call on, so take note of the advantages and potential problems your group faced and what your own role was in using or resolving them.

We'll be looking in more detail later at how the audience can see good (or bad) teamwork in action, but it's safe to say that group responsibility needs to be established right from the start so that there is no doubt that this is a real team effort and not just a series of short presentations by individuals. Teamwork will start to matter in the choice of topic for the presentation.

Sometimes teams are allowed to choose their own topics, within the parameters set by the lecturer, but more frequently the lecturer will suggest a range of topics from which the groups can choose. These will almost always be huge topics that couldn't possibly be covered in a presentation and so one of the first tasks of the team is to decide what aspect they want to talk about.

Choosing the subject

The team now needs to get together in order to agree their topic and start planning. This isn't always as easy as it sounds because sometimes people have strong ideas about what they do or don't want to tackle. It's useful to have a series of questions to discuss before making a decision:

- Is your first choice too popular, so that several groups might be using the same material or, worse, the same contacts?
- Has anyone in the group had work experience of any of the possible topics?
- Has anyone got a contact, perhaps a family member, who works in this area?
- Can anyone already see the possibilities of these topics: for instance how one of them might be tackled in an interesting or original way?
- Are there implications for the group in any of these topics? For instance, would travel (and therefore time and money) be involved?

If these questions are considered before any decision is made, you may find that it has more or less made itself: it's obvious that the group has more to offer if it chooses one topic rather than the others. But the discussion has to be fair: nobody should be saying that they won't work with one topic or trying to bully the group into a particular choice. It's always easier to 'lose' such a debate if you feel that your point of view has been thoroughly considered and it's essential that everybody cooperates once an initial decision has been made.

Still, it may be wise to have a second choice in case the first proves difficult. This has the advantage that if there's a division of opinion, one possibility isn't ruled out too quickly.

Limiting the topic

As we suggested, the topic you've agreed on is likely to be much too big for a short presentation and one of the most important stages in the preparation is choosing the aspect you're going to work on. Let's look at a group of management students, for example, who've been asked to look at recruitment policy, with special reference to the retail industry. This is a huge topic on which books might be written and it's obviously impossible in terms of a 20-minute presentation. So the group will need to decide what is possible: realistically, it might be graduate recruitment in a particular store which is perhaps part of a nationwide chain. Does any member of the group have relevant experience as a result of a holiday or weekend job or work experience? Perhaps someone has worked for a while in John Lewis or Marks & Spencer and can therefore provide a contact for information-gathering, if possible during a visit to the local store. The group needs to make clear at the beginning of the presentation what the limits of their presentation are, so that everybody knows that they're not looking at recruitment in general but giving a short case study about a particular level of recruitment in a specific store.

It's generally true that the narrower the focus of the subject covered, the better the presentation. We can imagine what would happen if our example group tried to talk about recruitment policies in the retail industry as a whole. They would have to resort to general statements that the audience could probably think of for themselves. It's the specific instances which produce original comments or interesting examples. Always look critically at your subject to see how it can be limited.

The group as a whole must be happy with the decisions it makes. If one student feels that he or she had a better idea and nobody listened, resentment will build up and the individual concerned may be reluctant to share the work. Of course, you can't please everyone, but you can try to ensure that everyone has taken part in the discussion and accepts the decision.

Gathering the information

This book can't suggest all the ways in which you might collect information for your presentation: it depends very much on your subject and the time available. However, many student presentations are based in part on information gathered through interviews and it's worth looking briefly at the communication issues involved (not how you get a representative sample, which is outside our scope!).

If you need to interview someone, give him or her as much notice as possible and send an email to confirm the agreed date, time and place. Don't necessarily send the whole group: two people can share the interviewing, but if there are half a dozen, the person being interviewed might feel overwhelmed, and almost certainly the interviewers will get in each other's way. However, the whole group has responsibility for preparing the questions. Allow plenty of time for this: don't jump from one aspect of the subject to another, but plan follow-up questions so that you get information in some depth. Questions that require a 'yes' or 'no' answer don't produce much information, while 'What do you do about . . . ?' or 'How would you tackle . . . ?' may lead to some useful examples. Your contact might want advance notice of your questions and you could email a list of them when they have been planned. Indeed, although there are obvious advantages in talking face to face, if your contact is very busy, he or she might prefer to carry out the whole interview by email, with you sending the questions and the contact adding the responses. This has the advantage of saving your time, too!

If you go on a visit, always make notes. It can be quite difficult to write notes when an individual is showing you round, but if you don't, you simply won't remember enough. This is especially true of any statistics you're given. Figures are always hard to get right, so if your contact tells you the percentage of graduate recruits still with the company after two years, check that you've got the figure right: 'You did say . . . didn't you?' Your attention to detail will be appreciated. You might even be able to borrow some visual aid material from the organisation, which can be very useful; never, of course, take a camera without asking in advance whether you may use it.

Ask how much time you can have and plan your questions accordingly. Arrive promptly and never overstay your welcome – your contact is busy and has already been generous in agreeing to see you. A brief letter or email of thanks afterwards is always appreciated.

Visit checklist

You are preparing to visit a local company to obtain information for your presentation. Have you:

- ❑ discussed the visit and what you want to achieve with the whole group?
- ❑ arranged a suitable date and time by discussion with your contact and agreed how long the interview should last?
- ❑ confirmed the arrangements by email?
- ❑ thought about the questions you want to ask and discussed them?
- ❑ considered the possibility of borrowing visual aids or asked if you might use a camera?
- ❑ decided how many of you, and who, should go?
- ❑ prepared note-taking material and asked permission if you want to record the information?
- ❑ arranged who will write to thank your contact afterwards?

Group image

Part of your preparation is deciding on the image you want to present. How formal is your presentation? If it's comparatively informal, perhaps a seminar presentation, then as long as you look clean and tidy, nobody is likely to complain. However, on some courses, especially in the sciences, engineering, and so on, you may be required to be as professional as possible. The occasion will be seen as very formal, as near to an industrial standard as it can be. In that case, the group should discuss how they should dress and where they should sit.

Formal dress may be difficult for impoverished students, but the group needs to make as much of a united effort as possible. If one person in a group wears a smart business suit and another wears jeans and a T-shirt, there's no sense of group identity. Nobody will suggest that you rush out to buy a suit, but you might be able to compromise on appropriately smart outfits. If you possibly can, wear shoes rather than trainers. This isn't just for the sake of your appearance, but because you will stand in a more upright, balanced way if you're wearing shoes; trainers suggest casual wear and you're more likely to slouch if you're wearing them. Generally, if you make some effort to look professional, you will make a good first impression on the audience and you will feel more professional in yourself – and confidence, as we've said, is important in making a good presentation.

No sense of group identity . . .

● The venue

Examine the room in which you'll be presenting. Where will the equipment be? Where will you stand when you're speaking, and where should you and your colleagues sit when you're not? It's rarely sensible to stand when someone else is talking, as you will distract attention from the speaker and you may fidget. It isn't easy to stand still when you have no role to play. Make sure that there are enough chairs for everyone and that you sit in the order in which you're going to speak so that it's easy for you to get up and move into position and sit down when you finish. The chairs must be in the audience's view, as you're still an integral part of the presentation, but not so close to the screen that they present a series of obstacles to the speaker! It's best to place them at an angle rather than in a straight line facing the audience, because if you catch the eye of the same person repeatedly as you sit there, one or both of you will want to laugh. Plan the layout of the room in advance so that you don't have to worry about it at the time and, if you possibly can, rehearse there.

Venue checklist

You are looking at the room in which you will make your presentation. Ask the following questions:

- ❏ Is it the right size for the numbers who will come?
- ❏ Where is the screen and any other fixed equipment?
- ❏ Where will you put your equipment?
- ❏ Are there sockets or will you need an extension lead?
- ❏ Where will you stand to speak?
- ❏ Where will the rest of the group be sitting?
- ❏ Are there any obstacles for the audience or can they see/hear well?
- ❏ Where are the light switches? Can you dim the lights if necessary?
- ❏ Are there blinds if you need them?
- ❏ Can you see a clock to check the timing?

At an early meeting of your group, you'll have started to plan a rehearsal schedule, to give everyone as much notice as possible of the times they need to note in their diaries. As soon as you feel that you have enough material, get together and plan who is going to give which section of the talk and in what order. Don't leave this too long. It might seem to be far too early to make these decisions, but you need to see where any problems might occur and agree about how to overcome them.

Preliminary rehearsal checklist

You are about to try out your presentation, although there are still decisions to be made. Make sure that you consider these aspects:

- ❏ Has everyone turned up? If not, contact those who are missing, as you need the whole group to rehearse together.
- ❏ Have you ordered the equipment for this and future rehearsals?
- ❏ Are you in the venue for your presentation or a similarly sized room?
- ❏ Is the room organised, as far as possible, as it will be for the event itself?
- ❏ Have you decided who will be responsible for the visual aids?
- ❏ How will you make the visual aids consistent in style and colour?
- ❏ Are you confident about the order in which you will speak?
- ❏ Are you all using the same form of notes?
- ❏ If you find, as you probably will, that your presentation is likely to be too long, can you all agree about the cuts to be made?

● Organising the group

You have most of your material, so now you have to organise who says what and in what order. Don't leave this stage too late, as each individual will want to work on his or her section and see how it fits into the whole. We mentioned earlier the importance of dividing the presentation according to the different aspects of the topic and deciding an appropriate amount of time for each, rather than crudely dividing the time available by the number of speakers.

Look at the skills of your group. Don't give the introduction to someone who has a soft voice and a retiring personality – you want to capture the audience's attention right from the start. You might want to give this role to someone with experience of acting or speaking to an audience, if it's possible. It's usually a good thing if the first speaker also ends the presentation, as this gives a sense of unity, of binding the whole topic together. It also means that you can use your strong speaker again for a memorable ending. Audiences tend to remember what they hear first and what they hear last, and it's wise to use this fact by giving a good speaker a key message to put across.

You will now have to organise your material, ensuring that all members of the group know which section they are responsible for and how their part fits into the whole. Not surprisingly, a presentation has a beginning, a middle and an end. The middle may, of course, be subdivided and presented by more than one person, but the overall structure must be logical and should flow smoothly. We'll discuss each part in turn.

● Structuring the presentation

The introduction

The beginning (and, as we've suggested, the end) of a presentation is the section that the audience takes particular note of, as their level of concentration is high. A good introduction gives time for listeners to settle and get themselves ready to hear the speaker, before you start giving the essential information in a way which catches their attention. Let's look at this in more detail.

An audience always wants to be sure who the speakers are. Unless you know that every single person in front of you knows your names (remembering that there might be invited members of staff who haven't taught you), make sure that you introduce yourselves at the beginning of your talk. (This includes the speaker, who sometimes forgets to introduce himself or herself.) You might want to list your names on a slide so that they are clear. If you do this, make sure that the names are in the order in which you speak. Then announce your subject and explain the structure of your presentation, for example: 'First, I'll describe . . . then my colleague Ben will discuss . . . Tim will cost this for you . . . and Tina will tell you about possible future developments before I sum up.'

This structure, which we can think of as the 'storyline', is very important. It reassures the audience about the logical coverage of the topic, lets them know who will handle which aspect and helps them to remember. From time to time, you will remind the audience of this structure: 'So we've looked at . . . now I'll ask Tim to tell you about the cost implications.' Smile at Tim as you say this and he should smile back and thank you. This is one of the main ways in which you can show teamwork: good handovers suggest that you each know what the others are going to say and that you've rehearsed together. Members of the audience carry the overall pattern, the storyline, in their heads and mentally attach the information to each stage. This gives them a logical sequence of information, which in turn helps their recollection of it afterwards. Remind the audience of the length of your presentation in your introduction (even if they know, they'll be glad to be reassured that you do) and tell them when they can ask questions.

All this preamble is essential, not just because it gives the audience useful information, but also because it allows them a moment or two to settle down. At the start of a presentation, people are checking whether they can see, hear, be comfortable. They're also assessing you, the speakers, to see how professional you are. If you begin giving them information immediately, they won't be quite ready and will miss the first thing you say. If you tell them these useful but not critical details, they will have time to settle, so that by the time you are ready to start talking about your topic, they are ready to listen.

Now start positively. Too many presentations begin in a hesitant, even apologetic, way, so that the audience starts to lose confidence before the speaker has said very much. Always smile at your audience and, when you've given them the preamble, make a strong beginning, with information that you know will catch their attention. Incidentally, you will have noticed how often the word 'you' came up in the little example of the introduction given above. Audiences like to feel involved and addressing them directly in this way helps to make them feel part of the occasion and so to listen more attentively.

Team support

Audiences are also helped by the obvious interest of the team itself. The group members who aren't speaking at any point must focus their attention on the speaker. This not only helps the audience to concentrate, but also ensures that each of you is listening carefully in case the speaker gets into any sort of difficulty, for instance missing out something important or making a point that you were supposed to make later. If this happens, don't look alarmed or irritated and don't interrupt the speaker. Such things can be the result of nerves and, provided that you have noticed, you may be able to help without attracting the audience's attention, by making the point missed or choosing different words to make your point so that it isn't obvious that it's been made already (a certain amount of repetition in a presentation doesn't matter anyway). If other members of the group fidget or look at their notes or, worst of all, whisper to each other, attention will be distracted from the speaker. This is unfair and also shows that the members of the team have little regard for one another. While you are in the audience's view, sit upright and look as if the section of the talk being presented is the most fascinating thing you've ever heard. (It's especially important to remember this when you've given your part of the presentation. Don't be tempted to sigh with relief that it's over, flop onto your chair and look exhausted.)

The low point

As the presentation proceeds, the level of audience concentration is likely to fall, and about two-thirds of the way through, it reaches its low point. You might like to arrange to move to the next speaker now, as a change of speaker adds variety and so helps concentration. You might use some powerful visual aids to revive the audience's attention. A small but useful technique is to ask the audience a question and then answer it yourself: the audience is suddenly aware that it has been invited to suggest an answer and starts concentrating anxiously, but, before it gets really worried, the answer is given by the speaker.

Humour

Sometimes this low point is seen as an opportunity for humour. This is very dangerous. If you can't time a humorous comment well, it falls flat. Humour can offend in ways we hadn't considered and it's a distraction from the serious message you're giving. We're not saying 'Don't ever use humour.' Sometimes it can be very effective, but it's tricky and needs to be well prepared. Off-the-cuff humour just isn't worth trying. If it goes wrong, you may find it extremely hard to get the audience's concentration back to you and your message.

The conclusion

Towards the end of the presentation, there's a moment when a high level of attention can be reached again, provided that the audience knows that the speaker is drawing to a close. When you say, 'Finally', or 'In conclusion', they suddenly realise that if they don't concentrate now, they will have lost the end of the talk. For a few moments, therefore, you have a high level of concentration once more. Don't waste this opportunity. Think back to your key message, the point you most want them to remember, and say it again in a slightly different way. When you really reach the end, don't peter out or say one of the irritating things that speakers sometimes say if they don't know how to finish, such as 'That's it', 'That's the end' or 'That's all we've got time for.' Simply pause, thank the audience for listening and ask for questions.

● Rehearsals

Rehearsals will be crucial to the success of your presentation, so plan them early and do your best to see that everyone turns up. We gave you some hints about timing earlier (pp. 79–81), but it's worth repeating that you can't get the timing right if you don't rehearse together. At the first full rehearsal you'll usually find that the presentation overruns and you need to decide together where to make cuts. The speaker whose part of the talk is affected needs to be clear about what is to be cut and why. This is also your chance to make sure that you've covered the subject sensibly between you and that the different sections are in a logical order. Ask each other whether you're speaking at the right speed and whether you can be heard (pp. 13–15). Check that you're all using the same form of notes and that your visual aids are consistent. Allow a minimum of three full rehearsals – more if you can possibly manage it. Don't worry if you feel that it's all going a bit stale after a lot of rehearsal: having the audience in front of you will make all the difference.

Final rehearsal checklist

You are about to go through your group presentation for the last time before you give it to your audience. Use this checklist to make sure that you've considered every aspect that will affect your success:

- ❏ Are you sure that the different sections are in a logical order?
- ❏ Does every member of the group know what he or she is going to say?
- ❏ Is there a strong introduction and conclusion?
- ❏ Is everyone familiar with everyone else's section?
- ❏ If someone were taken ill at the last minute, are you confident that the presentation could go ahead?
- ❏ Are you all familiar with and confident in your visual aids?
- ❏ Are you all at ease with the equipment?
- ❏ Is the timing now right; that is, a little shorter than the time you've been allowed?
- ❏ Have you all agreed what would be left out if there were a timing emergency?
- ❏ Can everybody be heard clearly?
- ❏ Will the speaker and the rest of the group be visible to the audience throughout the presentation?
- ❏ Are you all using notes effectively?
- ❏ Are the handovers between speakers smooth and courteous?
- ❏ Have you planned answers to likely questions?
- ❏ Who will receive the questions and coordinate the group's response?

● Answering questions

Question time in a group presentation requires careful organisation. It's sometimes the part that the audience and, oddly, the presenters like best because you can be sure that the audience is really interested, as it is they who are setting the agenda. On the other hand, it's sometimes dreaded because it's the session when you don't know what's going to happen. This shouldn't be the case.

If you work hard, you will be able to forecast many of the questions you're likely to be asked. Think about what you're going to say and what people are likely to want to know. Rehearse in front of one or two colleagues and ask them what they think the questions will be. Ask yourself if you've given a lead at any point by saying, for example, 'It's an interesting question that we'd like to know more about' or 'We think there might be more implications, which we're only just beginning to realise.' Such comments could well provoke a response: 'May I suggest an answer to the question' or 'What sort of implications are you referring to?' Notice that the first of these isn't a question, it's a member of the audience helping you out, but who will remember that? In an academic setting, you might even ask the audience if anyone can suggest an answer when you can't, especially if there are research students or staff present. Of course, if no one knows the answer, you will have to say so; it certainly would be unwise to bluff.

Don't become agitated if you all find the questions difficult. This is an academic occasion after all, and you're not going to lose a contract because you didn't know the answer. If the topic is one that members of staff present are researching, they may find it quite hard to judge your level of knowledge, or they may get so excited about the subject that they're almost talking to themselves or each other rather than to you. Very occasionally, someone might be deliberately aggressive, perhaps to see how well you cope. Whatever the situation, you will get credit for keeping calm and saying very courteously that you don't know the answer but that you found the question interesting. Your questioner may give you more information afterwards, if you've shown an interest in knowing, and nobody would expect you to have all the answers. Having said that, if you've prepared properly, you will be able to handle at least some of the questions between you, which will increase your confidence.

The question and answer session is one of the key times for showing your excellent teamwork. The easiest way to organise it is to let your last speaker take the questions and pass them on to the appropriate member of the group. Occasionally, he or she might want to give the answer, but this shouldn't happen too often because it must clearly be a group activity. Decide in advance who's going to deal with which type of question, although this will probably be obvious from the section of the presentation that each of you has given. Sometimes a question won't fall clearly into any category, and the person effectively in charge of the session will have to take a moment to decide who should answer. This gives the team valuable thinking time. It's also useful, after you've answered a question, to look at the rest of your group and ask if anyone wants to add anything. If they do, the audience is given extra information; if they don't, at least you've shown how much you think of yourself as part of a team.

Never interrupt each other or a member of the audience. This can happen because of nerves (for more help with nerves, see pp. 30–2) or because someone is overanxious to give an answer. A question can change course partway through and, if you answer too quickly, you may find that the questioner says, 'But that isn't what I was going to ask!' This is embarrassing, as the speaker has been seen to be discourteous. In the same way, you might feel that you can give a better answer than the one your colleague is giving. This might be true, but you must wait until you have an opportunity to speak. If you seem to be criticising another member of the team, that too destroys the impression that you are a united team, as of course you are.

Take your time in giving an answer, especially if the question was a difficult one. Nobody will mind if you pause for thought. Indeed, you will get credit for having the confidence to think before you speak. It's also possible to say something in answer to a question that you regret when it's too late, such as, rather pointedly, 'I said that in my talk!' Members of the audience can't be expected to concentrate on every word you said, and it's quite possible that the point was simply missed or that the questioner was particularly interested and would like to hear more. Don't appear to put someone down just because they missed a few words of your talk.

It's unlikely in a student presentation that there will be no questions, especially if there are members of staff present. Should this happen, you might want to use a question of your own to generate some discussion, perhaps asking if anyone has any ideas about, or experience of, something you mentioned in the talk. This might be just enough to get questions going, especially as people are often reluctant to ask the first question. When you ask for questions, there's usually a pause before someone feels ready and confident enough to ask.

The presentation isn't over until the next group has taken your place, or either you or the audience are outside the door. Don't spoil the impression of teamwork at the last minute by, for instance, looking crossly at someone who didn't speak as well as in rehearsal. You have all made an effort and you will all do even better next time, so smile encouragingly at one another and congratulate yourselves on a job well done.

Answering questions checklist

You are part of a group preparing a presentation and now you are thinking about the question and answer session. Discuss the following aspects:

❏ What questions do you think you might be asked?
❏ Have you guided the audience at any point by saying something like, 'There's more to that, of course, and we'll be happy to answer questions about it later'?
❏ How are you going to receive the questions? Who will be responsible for taking and allocating each question?
❏ Are you hoping that each person will answer on his or her own section of the talk? Will you remember to include everyone in this session?
❏ Are you all going to stand up to answer questions or will each person who has an answer to give stand up to give it?
❏ Are you sure that you will all remember that you are a team, and must look like a team, just as much when answering questions as in the main presentation?

Top Tips
- Get to know one another and identify the skills available
- Divide the time according to the subject, not the number of speakers
- Agree your topic and limit it rigorously – you haven't time to say much
- Structure your presentation and make sure that it has a strong beginning and end
- Plan visits and interviews and make lots of notes
- Check the venue to decide where you and your equipment should be placed

- Rehearse together several times, if possible in the venue for the presentation
- Make sure that everyone is introduced to the audience
- Listen to each other with enthusiasm – the audience will notice if you don't
- Organise how you are going to answer questions – decide who will deal with what
- Treat your audience with courtesy, however irritating they may be
- Support one another every moment of your time in front of the audience

6 Speaking as a Student Representative

This chapter helps you to

▶ assess whether it's right for you to stand for election
▶ gather public opinion and decide its strengt[
▶ put your case clearly and in a balanced way
▶ listen before responding briefly and effectively
▶ speak at an open day in a positive, helpful way
▶ plan where and wher to speak to a group touring the campus
▶ speak to new student in a friendly and encouraging way

An important part of student life, as we've seen, is time spent in clubs and societies, meeting a range of people from varied backgrounds, taking different subjects from your own, and such experience may be invaluable for your future, both at work and in your social life. It should feature in your personal development documentation, as it will help to show you how your own interests are evolving and it will almost certainly be relevant to your preparation for a job interview (see Chapter 8). You may also want to be influential in your group by becoming a student representative, acting as an intermediary between other students and staff in your department or your hall of residence. In this chapter, we'll look at what is involved.

● **Choosing to stand**

You have been at your college or university for a while and have been active in discussions, both as part of your course and at student meetings of various kinds. Now you are thinking of playing a more critical part in the life around you and wonder how this is to be achieved. Look at the roles that appeal to you, talk to people who've held office in the past and decide on the area in which your interests lie: would you, for instance, like to represent other students in matters that concern your course or would you prefer to move away from study and be a representative of the students in your hall of residence?

Once you've found an area in which you would like to make an impact, consider what you see as your main attributes. Are you good at meeting a range of people and talking to them in a friendly way about their concerns? Do you think that the group of people you spend much of your time with would be likely to support you? Why does this possibility appeal to you? Try to be honest about whether you want to be noticed (not necessarily a bad thing!) or whether you are really concerned about particular issues and want to have the chance to change things. Both may, of course, be true. Talk to other people, especially those who might vote for you, to make sure that you have enough support to make it sensible to put yourself forward: it would be embarrassing to discover too late that another highly popular figure wanted the same job and you were unlikely to get many votes.

It may be that you are someone whom people listen to and some of your friends have suggested you stand for office as a student representative. This is flattering, of course, but don't assume that you should automatically say yes. Whether it's your own idea to assume this responsibility or someone else's, it's wise to take a little time to think through the implications of what you would be taking on. How is your work going? Do you have difficulty in meeting deadlines? Do you have an important exam looming? These might be good reasons for deferring the opportunity. There's also a potential problem in that you may be asked to represent various different bodies and there could be a conflict of interest between them; you could be spreading your activities too widely, so that it's difficult to find the time for all you've taken on. At the same time, you might feel that it's worth getting this experience early in your course, either because you are thinking of representing others at a higher level in the future or because later, when you are facing major exams, your time will be even more precious.

Don't just think of your current workload. Will you have more to do next term or later in the academic year? If you are elected, how long will you be the representative? In most cases, it will be for the whole academic year, so you shouldn't take a decision lightly just because at present you don't have a heavy workload. Would it be possible either to share the work with another student or to hand over halfway through the year? It might be worth asking if either of these is possible.

Time is an important consideration and you need to assess the time involved carefully. Don't just think of the time you would spend at meetings; you would need to talk informally to the people whose interests you are representing and to prepare your case before you go to a formal meeting. How far could you use email as a means of communication rather than face-to-face discussions or meetings? Find out from previous holders of the office, and also ask them whether – as is increasingly likely – they used Facebook.

You will probably create a Facebook group for your campaign, as you will be able to reach a far bigger number of potential voters that way and will also be able to set out your case in much more detail. You might also think of having a link from Facebook to a website that you've created especially for the campaign. This would give you an impressive image, but it would take a lot of your time. You would have to be sure that it looked professional – people are used to looking at websites and they expect a high standard.

Let's assume that you want to use Facebook to reach as many potential voters as possible. What do you have to keep in mind?

- Your site will need to be as professional as possible and at the same time friendly and appealing. Remember that your tutors and potential employers are likely to look at it (Horrors! – but see Chapter 8).
- Friendly and approachable are good; amateur is not. Pictures of you on the floor of the union bar at the end of a fun evening are unlikely to win you many votes! Positions are hotly contested, and you need to appear professional and competent.
- You will probably have what you hope is a winning strategy and a slogan. Use them but remember that voters will want to know much more about your views. Make sure that you include enough information for them to be able to decide to support you.
- Try not to be heavily swayed by friends as you create a group. They like you and want to support you, of course, and they may love some of your more quirky attributes. Making much of these on Facebook might suggest that you are more concerned with your friends than with the wider body of students you want to represent.
- Be careful not to offend anyone as you prepare your group. If you do, they will tell other people and you'll risk losing a good number of voters. It's not always easy to see that you might offend, so ask someone whose judgement you trust to take a good look before you allow other people to access it.
- Your opponents have supporters too and they may leave messages on the site that are less than complimentary. However irritating this might be, it's probably best to ignore them. If you allow yourself to get embroiled in long arguments or respond too quickly and too abrasively, you may live to regret it.

Being asked to represent other students is an attractive idea and good for the ego, but if you take on many such jobs, you may end up by doing none of them thoroughly and may get a reputation for not carrying out your promises. Being a student representative will look good on your CV, but not if you have represented half a dozen different interests at the same time. All these considerations should be weighed up before you take a deep breath and say yes.

Decision making checklist

You are considering standing for election as a student representative. Have you sufficiently considered the following:

- ❑ Why are you thinking of this? What different motives are you aware of?
- ❑ Have you talked to friends and others about the possibility?
- ❑ How much support, realistically, are you going to get?
- ❑ Would you be taking the job on for the whole academic year?
- ❑ Have you tried to assess the probable workload as realistically as possible?
- ❑ Would it be feasible to share the responsibility with another student?
- ❑ Would you enjoy the responsibility or are you thinking only of your CV?

Let's assume that you have agreed to represent your fellow students at departmental or hall meetings. These are likely to fall into two categories: open meetings, at which any student can raise a topic of concern, and departmental/hall management committee meetings, at which the subjects raised are discussed with members of staff who are empowered to make a decision or pass on your concerns to higher authorities.

● Open meetings

An open meeting is an occasion on which your fellow students can make their interests and concerns known to you, their representative. The session could be general – various issues would be raised without your prior knowledge – or interim – called specifically to discuss a single issue, such as security in a hall of residence after a case of theft had been reported. In the former, it's hard for you to prepare for the meeting in any depth, although it's a good idea to ask around among a representative selection of your peers to discover whether any particular issues are likely to come up. You may well be able to get a good sense of the topics which people feel most strongly about and, more importantly, how much support there is for the point of view expressed.

Be prepared for a good deal of noisy discussion. Students aren't always used to expressing their ideas in an orderly way and, if they feel very strongly, they may become emotional and perhaps talk for too long, making it difficult for other people to join in. In the example of hall security that we mentioned earlier, you can imagine that emotions might run high, with many students wanting to complain or make suggestions, not all of them realistic. You need to keep calm and be ready to intervene courteously if you feel that the point of view expressed, or the discussion, is getting out of hand. An open meeting needs to have a time limit which is known to everyone and strictly observed. If necessary, suggest that it reconvenes after a few days. This gives people time to cool off and allows you time to discuss the problem with individuals. When you've clarified your own thinking, try to find a few people who feel the same way as you do, so that when you have to decide what action should be taken, you will have some support.

There is another important consideration: people become very irate if they feel they aren't being listened to. Give time and effort to your 'constituents', so they know that their point of view has been taken seriously, even if you don't agree with it or it's voted out of the discussion. Again, sounding students out on an individual basis shows how seriously you take your role as a representative, and this might be done by email rather than by going out to find people. You will gain a good deal of time by electronic rather than face-to-face discussion, as you can avoid the lengthy conversation or the invitation to the bar. However, don't just rely on email, useful though it is; sometimes you need to mix with other students to make sure that they recognise you as someone who is friendly and approachable. (See also the section of Chapter 7 headed 'Chairing meetings', which will give you additional advice.)

Open meeting checklist

You are preparing to chair an open meeting. Have you:

- ❑ found out, as far as you can, what topics are likely to be discussed?
- ❑ arranged a time limit for the meeting and planned to keep to it?
- ❑ listened to as many different points of view as possible and thought about how you will respond if they're presented?
- ❑ used email to discuss how people feel about the subjects that might arise?
- ❑ prepared yourself so that you will remain calm and in control?

● Committee meetings

Before you represent the views of the open meeting at a committee meeting, you will need to prepare carefully. Gather as many facts and figures as you can. In the example of security at a hall of residence, find out if there are any obvious features that need to be drawn to everyone's attention, such as a window being left open when the room wasn't occupied. Ask the views of the hall warden and the police: they have seen it all before and can share their experience of where the problems might be and what solutions might work in the future. Find out what has been done about security in the past, and, if you can, what ideas have been rejected. You don't want to suggest something which has previously been tried and abandoned. Ask other students if they can think of ways in which security might be strengthened and perhaps ask whether the hall managers agree that the local crime prevention officer might come to give a talk on security. Make sure that you are in possession of the facts before you have to discuss the issue with members of the committee.

It's not only important to gather information, it's also necessary to prepare what you want to say. You will be talking to professional people, many of them highly articulate and trained in logical thinking, and you will fare badly if you don't have your case well prepared and well argued. Think of the main points you want to make and have some notes available so you don't forget. Try to have a small number of supporting arguments to put forward in favour of your point, but remember that overkill is possible: you can produce so many arguments that people listening may think that you haven't seen both sides of the question. Be prepared to concede that another point of view is reasonable and perhaps, if you can, adopt an aspect of your opponent's argument and incorporate it into your own. Sounding dogmatic or aggressive will weaken your case and make people listen more sympathetically to other people. Don't waffle and don't talk for too long. Make your points clearly and briefly, using the techniques described in Chapter 2 – projecting your voice effectively and supporting what you say with appropriate NVC. It's essential to be as unemotional as you can, however strongly you feel about the subject. A calm, courteous, logical presentation is likely to carry the most weight.

Think about the possibility of using visual aids. You might need to introduce your topic with a short talk: would it be worth having a few facts and figures on acetate to use with an overhead projector or on a data projector slide? A flipchart can be useful for generating discussion within a small group: you could write up the ideas that are put forward, as seeing them encourages people to take them seriously and, of course, remember them. (See Chapter 3 for advice on using visual aid equipment.)

Above all, listen. The ability to listen well is rare and valuable: people generally prefer either to talk or switch off rather than listen carefully to what is being said. If you can develop the ability to listen productively, you will in turn tend to be listened to. It's useful to be able to say, 'I agree with Susan, but I think that . . .' or 'That's a very good point and perhaps I hadn't considered it sufficiently.' This kind of comment makes the speaker concerned feel good, and everybody else will notice that you are listening and responding to other people. They are then more ready to direct their comments to you, listen to your replies and give you time to make your own points fully.

Time is of great importance to people on a committee, especially if they have other responsibilities in the hall or department and other meetings to attend. In the next chapter, we'll look at chairing and speaking at meetings, but it's worth saying now that you need to be aware of the possible time constraints other people are facing. If the discussion stops more quickly than you want, and you didn't have time to present all your arguments as fully as you'd like to, accept that you might have tried to say too much and need to be more concise in the future. This will come with practice.

If the body on which you're sitting is based in your department rather than your hall, you will need to be particularly skilful at deciding what is or is not within your area of responsibility. The most important person in most departments is said to be the departmental secretary. Even if this is an exaggeration, it's certainly worth talking to him or her about what has happened in the past and what the etiquette of such meetings is. You might also find out without asking who the most argumentative or most persuasive members of staff are! Mature or postgraduate students might also be useful sources of information and provide helpful hints on how to approach difficult topics.

Inevitably, staff members of the committee will have other concerns, for instance about the content as well as the conduct of exams, which affect you and other students but which you will inevitably approach from a different point of view. Be sensitive about this. If you show an awareness, for instance, of the enormous amount of time staff spend marking exam papers and discussing the results, then they are more likely to take you seriously if you want to raise an issue about trial exam papers. A mock exam can be very useful to students, but it greatly increases the workload for staff and they may be unwilling to undertake such a task, however sympathetic they are to the need of students to prepare adequately and receive help and advice before they take major exams. You may be able to work out a compromise if you have shown that you can approach the question with respect for its implications. You might even think of a possible compromise in advance so that, if your request is not well received, you have something else to offer to your constituents – perhaps the possibility of an extra revision session in the skills centre or with a postgraduate student. Some areas of discussion, for instance disciplinary proceedings, will exclude you completely and, again, you need to accept this as inevitable in a meeting that includes professional teachers as well as student representatives.

Whatever its area of concern, the committee on which you sit will probably make decisions and issue recommendations, and part of your brief is to give feedback to the other students. It's as well to do this in a meeting or in an email sent to the whole group if possible so that everyone hears the same story and has an equal opportunity to ask questions. Try to avoid giving part of your message to friends or people who stop you to ask a question without giving a complete picture to everybody. You represent all of them, whether or not they agree with your point of view. Again, if you hold a meeting, prepare what you want to say, have notes with you and allow enough time for those who want to ask questions to do so. There are, of course, other ways of distributing information widely, such as through student union newspapers or a hall of residence newsletter. Writing an article in one of these outlets will take quite a bit of your time but you can reach people effectively and they have the opportunity to respond if they wish to do so.

You will have noticed how long all this procedure takes, which reinforces what we said earlier – being a student representative is a time-consuming job which shouldn't be undertaken by anyone who isn't ready to give the time and effort needed to do it well.

Committee meeting checklist

You have to represent the views of your constituents at a committee meeting. Have you prepared thoroughly in the following ways:

- ❑ Have you found out as much as you can about the topic you have to speak on? Did you talk to the appropriate authorities?
- ❑ Did you discuss the conduct of the meeting with the departmental secretary and other influential people?
- ❑ Have you checked relevant facts and figures as fully as you can?
- ❑ Are your arguments well prepared, logical and objective? Have you considered the opposing point of view sensitively?
- ❑ Have you made some notes to speak from?
- ❑ Are you prepared to listen to other points of view, modifying or changing your own if necessary?
- ❑ Have you considered using visual aids and prepared them if they're appropriate?
- ❑ How will you pass on the decisions of the meeting to your constituents?

● **High-level committees**

If you've been successful as a hall or department representative, you may want to volunteer to be a student member of a body which is influential in the life of the college or university, such as the senate or council. You may even think of doing so if you haven't had experience in a smaller or less influential body. Either way, you will be taking on a great deal of responsibility and the time involved will be even greater.

Perhaps the two aspects of such a role that are most frequently mentioned by staff representatives are that students must prepare adequately for meetings and put their point of view in a calm and logical way. Preparation is always important but in this case it may involve reading large amounts of paperwork, sometimes in educational jargon with which you might be unfamiliar. Don't feel demoralised if this happens, but do be ready to ask for help in good time so that you have a clear picture of the issues before you get to the meeting. Don't rely on last-minute inspiration – there will be too many knowledgeable people present who will be quick to realise if you haven't done your homework properly.

When you receive the agenda for the meeting, go through it carefully to decide which issues you might want to speak on and which are of no great importance from your point of view. If you want to speak, prepare your material well in advance, discuss the issue with other people to get their point of view, trying out your argument, and write notes for yourself, much as you would for a presentation. Look at your evidence and check how much of it is based on fact and how much on anecdotal reports; you need hard evidence if you are to convince these highly educated, articulate people of your point of view. Don't just repeat vague or unsubstantiated complaints – they will soon be dismissed.

At the meeting, listen carefully to other people in case they say something which will undermine what you planned to say or they produce an approach which you hadn't thought of. When you feel that it's the right moment for you to speak, don't be put off. Staff can sometimes sweep a student point of view aside, perhaps by using jargon or a lot of statistics: you need to stick to what you want to say and make sure that your voice is heard. It will be too late when the meeting is over and it's no good having regrets then that you didn't make the points you wanted to make.

There's also the danger that you might speak on impulse because you've been irritated or antagonised by something that has been said. You had no intention of speaking but on the spur of the moment you felt that you wanted to contribute. This isn't necessarily the wrong thing to do, but you run the risk of saying too much, showing that you don't know what you're talking about because you haven't done any homework, or saying something you later regret. The excitement of the meeting might lead you into difficulties which it wouldn't be easy to get out of and you might gain a reputation as someone who speaks before they think.

Never let your emotions get the better of you. Whatever the circumstances, as you speak, take care to be courteous towards other speakers, especially those you don't agree with, and stay resolutely calm even if you feel angry or upset by

Don't let your emotions get the better of you!

what is said. Your job is to put your case as logically, coherently and calmly as you can. If you succeed, you will make a good impression and, even if your point of view is defeated, people will be more ready to listen to you next time.

High-level meeting checklist

You are about to take part in a meeting of senior people, such as the university senate. Has your preparation included the following stages:

- ❏ Have you done your homework thoroughly, read all the papers you were sent and asked advice if something wasn't clear?
- ❏ Did you check the agenda for subjects on which you might want to speak?
- ❏ Are the points you want to make relevant, logical and fair and can you put them courteously and calmly?
- ❏ Have you made notes to speak from?
- ❏ Are you prepared to listen, and compromise if it seems the right thing to do?

● Open days

Part of your work as a student representative might be involvement in open days for your department or your hall of residence or as a students' union spokesperson. You will probably be asked to lead a group of twenty or so prospective students around the campus and, in the appropriate building, to speak to them about life within the college or university and answer their questions.

A tour of the buildings or campus is invaluable, as the prospective students have the chance to move around and get a general feel for the place. This can make a welcome break from being on the receiving end of a lot of information, much of which they will find difficult to remember. So make this part of your job as lively and enjoyable as you can, showing them sports facilities, attractive areas for walking and interesting buildings, perhaps including a reference to any unusual subject areas which other places of further or higher education don't have. Don't try to speak to the group while you're on the move, as some people won't be able to hear you clearly. Choose a good place to pause and talk for a few minutes, answer any questions and then move on. A few people will join you as you walk and will start a conversation. It's as well not to talk one to one, as others will feel excluded, but you should of course be friendly towards the small group you're walking with. Notice any comments they make which might be of more general interest and, next time you pause, pass them on to the rest of the group. ('Someone's just asked me about joining the leisure centre. Well, it's easy . . .')

The more formal talk you may have to give will need careful preparation, especially if there are parents present. Their concerns might be different from those of the prospective students: they are likely to be concerned about security on the campus, medical treatment if someone is ill, or how far students are chased up if they don't hand in their work on time. You will have to balance these genuine concerns with those of the young people themselves, who will be anxious to have a student's eye view. It won't be very long since you were in the same position yourself, so think back to the questions you wanted to ask. You might have had worries about being lonely, finding the work difficult or not being able to take part in some sporting activity you were keen on. The group you're speaking to will be just the same, so you need to reassure them. Don't make everything sound too easy – if it's the first time they've been away from home, their new life will present them with some challenges, all part of their adaptation to a more grown-up and independent existence. At the same time, practical advice about topics such as registering with the medical service or keeping a check on finances will almost certainly be helpful and will reassure the parents too.

You may want to describe the content of the course you are taking and explain the options that are possible and when choices have to be made. Don't try to give too much detail, and remember that it's likely a member of staff will be dealing with such issues later. It's better if the visitors are given a handout with an outline of the course so that you can refer to information that they can see in front of them. Allow plenty of time for questions but don't hesitate to say politely that you can't answer a particular question but that there will be an opportunity to put it to the appropriate person later on. As you answer, be positive and enthusiastic – your own interest in and enjoyment of the course will carry more weight than detailed information.

You are acting as an ambassador for your place of study and your course and if you sound bored, you can't expect them to go away with a good impression. Sometimes you may be asked to make a formal presentation to prospective students and their parents about your course and what it has to offer. Such a talk would probably take place before the open day and might be given at a local school or college. The same approach applies: think of the particular interests of both age groups and achieve a balance between them.

Don't minimise the difficulties. If, for instance, your course involves a year abroad, you can't hide the potential problems of language and culture barriers, and possible isolation, but you can still point to some of the positive aspects: the students will be in email and Facebook contact with tutors and friends and they will soon find that their speaking and comprehension improve so that they can make friends locally. Be bright and cheerful about the course and your place of study, and try not to allow a worried parent to make the whole tone of the occasion dismal instead of encouraging.

Open day checklist

You have been asked to be a student representative for your department on an open day. Have you prepared in the following ways:

- ❑ Have you planned a tour of the campus that is varied and interesting?
- ❑ Have you thought about what you will want to say at each stopping place? What questions are you likely to be asked?
- ❑ Is your more formal talk going to interest both prospective students and any parents who might be there?
- ❑ Have you prepared good notes and, if they are appropriate, visual aids?

Open day checklist (continued)

❑ Is your talk honest about any difficulties and reassuring as far as possible?

❑ Can you rehearse your talk in front of two or three colleagues?

❑ Are the details of your course on a handout that your audience can take away with them?

❑ Are you going to sound positive, cheerful and encouraging?

● Talking to new students

Talks to first-year students during their induction might be another part of your job. They have now made their decision to live in the same hall of residence or take the same course, and your role is to help them to feel that they have made the right choice and that their wellbeing is of concern to others. They need to feel that they belong. You are now likely to be giving more detailed information, but your enthusiasm is still important. If you have a particular role such as that of welfare officer for the students' union, you will be concentrating on topics such as accommodation or safety. Plan what you want to say, remembering that people's concentration span is short, they will have a lot of talks to listen to and it's better to put detail into a handout while you stress the aspects that are of special relevance. Take all questions seriously, even if they sound naive or pointless to you – they seem important to the student who asked them.

A greater challenge might be to make a similar presentation to international students on their arrival. They will all speak some English, of course, but they might not be used to hearing it spoken quickly and idiomatically. You will need to speak even more slowly than usual and try to articulate your words clearly (see pp. 13–15). Avoid expressions which seem absolutely clear to a native audience but which will sound odd to people whose first language isn't English: 'letting the cat out of the bag', for instance. You may want to produce more material in handout form and, if possible, use visual aids to help people to follow what you say. When you ask for questions, be prepared to ask for the question to be repeated if you can't understand it and perhaps to get help from another speaker if you still can't make it out. Remember that these students will be feeling particularly vulnerable, so your smile, friendly approach and obvious sympathy for any difficulty they are experiencing will be especially appreciated. If you can't answer their questions, suggest someone whom they should approach to get help and, if you feel that it's appropriate, have a word with any individuals who still need reassurance at the end of your talk.

The skills of making a successful presentation have been described in detail earlier in this book. Reread Chapters 2 and 3 before you start to plan what you will say but remember that, in speaking at an open day or to new students, you must appear friendly and approachable. This is likely to be much more influential than all the words of wisdom you can summon up.

Talking to new students checklist

You've been asked to speak to a group of new students during their induction. Have you:

- ❏ planned what you want to say and prepared notes and visual aids if appropriate?
- ❏ prepared a handout containing the detail that they won't remember from your talk?
- ❏ found out whether these are overseas students or not?
- ❏ planned to speak especially slowly and carefully if they are, avoiding colloquial expressions that might be puzzling?
- ❏ discussed with two or three friends any likely questions and how you should answer them?
- ❏ made a note of sources of further information that your audience might need?
- ❏ prepared yourself to be as approachable and friendly as you can?

Top Tips

- Be realistic about the time involved in being a representative
- People want to have their say – be prepared to listen
- Prepare thoroughly for any meeting – gather facts and opinions
- Plan well-ordered logical arguments and deliver them courteously
- Never speak before you think
- Remain calm and in control in spite of provocation
- At an open day, consider the interests of both new students and their families
- Be approachable and friendly – you were a new student yourself once

7 Speaking at Elections and Meetings

This chapter helps you to

- ▶ assess your potential support and the workload involved in taking office
- ▶ prepare short, bulletpoint speeches with a strong message
- ▶ handle a press interview effectively
- ▶ speak at a meeting with confidence and authority
- ▶ introduce a guest speaker in a clear and positive way
- ▶ prepare for a meeting that you're going to chair and plan the agenda
- ▶ guide the meeting in a firm, fair and friendly way
- ▶ feel confident that if you are in the chair, you are in control

In the previous chapter, we looked at some of the roles you might choose for your leisure time, such as representing other students on a range of bodies from a hall committee to a university senate. Now we're widening the theme to include a range of speaking occasions which you may or may not want to undertake during your student career.

We'll start with getting elected to office within your students' union or as chairperson of a society and being interviewed by a student newspaper, and then we'll discuss meetings in more detail. This won't involve 'written' aspects, such as the agenda and minutes, but it will include the responsibilities of committee members and those who chair meetings to prepare well and speak effectively so that the meeting runs as smoothly as possible. You may have already had some experience of these roles in your school or college, or in a club you belonged to before you came to further or higher education, but it's likely that you will now have a larger and perhaps more critical audience for these activities.

● Election to office

Before you stand for office in, for instance, the Students' Union, you will need to think carefully about your motives and time planning, much as we suggested in Chapter 6 when we discussed whether it was sensible to choose to be a student representative. The considerations we listed there, especially about time, apply to all positions of responsibility and, unless you would be in the fortunate position of having an automatic sabbatical year in which to carry out your duties, you need to make a rational decision about whether it's right to take such a step at the particular stage you've reached in your academic study.

If you decide to go ahead, you will need to prepare your case for election thoroughly, talking to the present and, if possible, a past holder of the position. The latter is particularly useful: the current official might feel that he or she has a vested interest in stressing the beneficial aspects of taking the post, while past officials can probably take a more dispassionate view. They may also be better placed to assess the longer-term advantages and disadvantages of the step you're considering.

The first stages of your campaign will involve talking to people or emailing them on an individual basis to assess how much support, both active and passive, you can command. This will take time, but it's essential: you don't want the humiliation of getting a tiny share of the votes, especially if the reason for this is that although lots of people said they'd support you, very few were willing to give the time and effort to campaign. As all politicians know, you need a good team behind you from the start.

When the campaign begins, you will probably find that much of the activity is in writing. You will need a manifesto, leaflets, posters, and so on – as much publicity material as you can afford. Towards the end, you're likely to start speaking to groups rather than individuals, and you'll need all the presentation techniques discussed in earlier chapters. Although much of this talking will be informal, you need to prepare as carefully as ever, checking in advance, as far as you can, the questions you're going to be asked. Under these circumstances, perhaps more than any others, you will need to remain calm and good-humoured, no matter what the provocation, and to think before you speak: the temptation to make a quick riposte at someone else's expense will be very strong at times, but if you give in to it, it might be disastrous.

On election day, you may be asked to make several short presentations. They may hardly be worth that name, maybe only two or three minutes at a time, but they will have a big impact on your success or failure. In such a short presentation, you can say very little and you can't afford to waste any time. Resist the temptation to speak quickly in order to say more: every word must be heard as every word counts. Say your name clearly and then put forward three short, focused points. Think of them as bullet points, starred for maximum impact, and presented slowly and dramatically so that everyone hears them and, with luck, remembers them. Sending your audience away with the three key messages of your manifesto is a lot better than trying to say a great deal in a short time and leaving no strong message at all. Finish by repeating your name to fix it in people's minds. Try this out, timing yourself carefully, and see if you can add one or two supporting sentences to each point. Time yourself again and, as usual, make sure that you're slightly under the time allowed, even if only by ten seconds.

This little speech may be followed by questions and answers, although again the time will be limited and the questions are likely to be general; the same may be asked of all the candidates and there'll be no time for difficult follow-up questions. How you deliver your speech and cope with the questions will be important: you have to give the impression of being at ease (especially if you're not) and of being friendly and approachable while carrying authority. It's a lot to ask of a three-minute talk so make sure that you rehearse it in front of a few friends until you can manage to convey all the right messages.

Three-minute election speech checklist

You are hoping to be elected to office in your Students' Union. The early stages have been completed, and you now face your three-minute talk. Have you considered all the following points and prepared as thoroughly as possible?

- ❑ Are you sure that you can be heard, even if there's a certain amount of background noise?
- ❑ Have you talked to some of the people who will be there and discussed the questions that you might get?
- ❑ Will a few friends be at strategic points in the crowd to encourage and support you?
- ❑ Have you identified a small number of key points that you want to make?
- ❑ Have you rehearsed, making these points slowly, clearly and emphatically, preferably in a large room with a friend at the back to check audibility and impact?
- ❑ Are you sure that you will remain calm, good natured and enthusiastic, even if you are heckled?

After the vote-counting, especially if you've won, you'll probably be interviewed by the student press or radio. That's rather different from giving a presentation, so we'll look at it separately.

● Speaking to the press

You will have had years of watching people speaking to an interviewer, especially on television, but you may never have realised how difficult it is until now! Nevertheless, it's worth thinking in advance about what you've seen, because it holds some good lessons for the beginner. Indeed, many of the people you will see are themselves new to the experience, which is why there's such a wide divergence between their performances. The main difference between them and you is that they have the advantage (or the disadvantage) of an expert interviewer who knows exactly how to encourage them to speak, and sometimes how to make them say things they might later regret. Your interviewer is a fellow student, who may or may not be good at the job. The danger is that he or she will try to shine at your expense. The good news is that they're more likely to want a good interview: that is, for you to give them information in an interesting and lively way.

You will have noticed that the interviewees who come over most poorly are those who fidget and won't look at the interviewer. It's difficult to feel that they mean what they say. There's also the category who mutter or speak too quickly, and, of course, the ones who don't answer the question but set off in a different direction and won't stop until they run out of breath. You aren't, of course, on television, but it's still a good idea to make the right impact on your interviewer by sitting reasonably still and making eye contact. If you also smile and look welcoming, you will be helping the questioner to feel at ease and in turn you will feel more comfortable. Plan what you want to say and, if you can, ask in advance what the line of questioning is going to be: even if you don't know the exact words, you can have thought about the type of answers you will want to give. Keep your answers short and let the interviewer come back with follow-up questions if he or she wants to do so. Stop and think before you speak if you suspect that the question has a catch in it, if necessary using the 'that's interesting, and I'd like to think about it for a moment' technique to give yourself time to consider your answer.

Try to answer the questions you're asked, unless you feel that they're too intrusive or unfair. Your interviewer is presumably intelligent enough to notice if you don't answer, and he or she may feel irritated if you seem unnecessarily evasive. Show enthusiasm for the issues you really care about, as you would in any presentation, and include facts and figures when it's reasonable to do so. Repeat the figures, as you want to be sure that they're being recorded accurately. If you haven't got the answer to a question with you but you know that you can get it quickly, offer to telephone or email it at the earliest opportunity. If you come across as helpful and friendly to your interviewer, this will probably be mentioned in the article, which will be good for your image. At the same time, if you really don't feel that you should answer a particular question, then don't, but smile and make your refusal as light and painless as possible.

Agree the length of the interview in advance, and, if possible, ask to see a draft of the article before it goes to print. You may notice that some of your answers have been 'tidied up' a little. As long as the meaning hasn't been changed, this is acceptable and indeed necessary: most of us will repeat words or say 'er' if we're speaking off the cuff, and your interview will read better if a good copy-editor has worked on it.

Press interview checklist

You've been elected (congratulations!) and now you are going to face an interview by a reporter from the student newspaper or radio. Think about how you are going to prepare for this:

❏ Agree the length of the interview and ask to see a draft of the article if possible.

❏ If the interviewer agrees, find out in advance what the main line of questioning will be.

❏ Take a few notes with any details that you want to mention but aren't sure you will remember, especially any figures.

❏ Be ready to encourage your interviewer: smile and make eye contact.

❏ Be prepared to refuse to answer any question you find inappropriate, but do so in a friendly way.

❏ If you need to think about a question, be ready to pause while you consider what you want to say: it's better than a rapid but unhelpful answer.

❏ You will have to face other interviews during your term of office, so it's in your interest to respond in as friendly and helpful a way as possible.

● **Speaking at meetings**

Part of your duties when you undertake any position of responsibility is speaking at and sometimes chairing meetings. You're likely to start by intervening to make a comment or perhaps a prepared statement or report on a subject you've been investigating. In many ways, this is a good beginning to your public-speaking career, as you get used to talking without the strain of standing up and making a formal presentation. Nevertheless, you can make an impact on the whole discussion if you prepare and speak well in a meeting.

There are two opportunities for doing this: one is to be the first speaker in a debate, introducing the topic and starting the discussion; the other is to intervene in response to what someone else has said. The former is much more like making a presentation, although the time limit is likely to be shorter (perhaps five minutes at most) and, unless you choose to use a visual aid such as a flipchart, you will be sitting at a table with everyone else. There is a potential difficulty with this: you can't easily see much of your audience.

At meetings people traditionally sit round a large table. This has obvious benefits in that they can all make notes, they have something to lean on and the person in charge can sit at the head. However, while it's easy enough to see the row of people opposite you, it's almost impossible, without standing up, to see those who are alongside you. This means that someone could be registering extreme annoyance at what you're saying, or nodding vigorously, and you probably wouldn't know. A horseshoe or circular formation is preferable, as much more eye contact is possible, but if you find yourself sitting on one side of the table, it may be worth pushing your chair back a little before you begin to speak. Other people on your side of the table will then tend to push their chairs back so that you may end up with a flat semicircle rather than a straight line. This is an improvement, but there's no simple answer to the problem of not easily seeing the audience. If the group is a big one, you might choose to stand to introduce the topic; once discussion has started, you will have to be seated like everybody else, but you will at least have had the advantage of seeing the response to your initial statement.

Flipcharts are useful visual aids at meetings, and if you use one, you will, of course, have a good reason for standing. If you need to quote facts and figures, especially the latter, write them on the second sheet of the flipchart before the meeting starts, so that you can reveal them at the right moment. A flipchart is a little less formal than an OHP or data projector, so it will tend to encourage discussion. You might continue to use it by listing the main suggestions about a controversial topic so that everyone can see all the possibilities in writing. The fact that the material on the flipchart is handwritten also encourages people to discuss it: it seems to be less finalised than a printed version. Presenting a statement or an introduction to discussion at a meeting is obviously similar to a presentation in that you can have visual aids, notes and a prepared and practised speech. Intervening is in some ways more difficult: you didn't know in advance that you were going to want to join in the discussion so you have to speak off the cuff. The potential hazards of this are obvious:

- you might not speak clearly or coherently
- you might not present your argument logically
- you might feel embarrassed or awkward
- you might say something you later regret.

If it's any consolation, most of us have fallen into these traps from time to time, and most of the people at your meeting will be sympathetic because they have, too. It's impossible totally to prevent such things happening, but there are ways of making them less likely, and we've listed some of them below.

Speaking at a meeting checklist

You are going to a meeting and you expect to join in the discussion. Remind yourself of the following guidelines:

- ❏ Before you start, quickly think of your main point and how you want to put it.
- ❏ If you speak slowly, you'll be listened to. Start in a friendly way, saying something like 'Mostly I agree with what my colleague said, although . . .', 'I think you've got a good point, but perhaps . . .', 'I wonder if you've thought about . . .' These are all ways of saying 'That's nonsense' without alienating the previous speaker.
- ❏ If you feel that you're not putting your point clearly, smile and admit it, then start again.
- ❏ Keep calm and pause from time to time. Don't speak without considering how you are going to say what you want to say.
- ❏ Smile and be courteous and people will be very forgiving. Never lose your temper or be sarcastic at someone else's expense.
- ❏ Be ready to admit it if you decide that the other person is probably right.

It's not easy to speak at a meeting at which there are senior people present, but if you get a reputation as someone who is thoughtful and courteous, people will listen and take your arguments seriously.

● Chairing meetings

In time, you may become the chairperson of a society or club and then you'll have the responsibility of organising and controlling meetings. It's a daunting thing to have to do, especially at first, but it's good experience and also looks good on your CV. However, before we look at general meetings, it's worth briefly discussing what happens when you take the chair to introduce a guest speaker.

Introducing guest speakers

From time to time, most organisations invite someone from outside the group to come and speak at a meeting. The guest may be another student who has a particular interest in and knowledge of a subject or someone who is well known and widely respected, perhaps nationally or even internationally.

Introducing such speakers can't be done off the cuff or with last-minute preparation. You will need to find out as much as you can about them, using the library, the internet and personal contact. Check on their exact position (remembering that a politician, for instance, might change jobs at a moment's notice in a government reshuffle), their official title, their publications and the authority with which they speak (for instance your speaker might be an eminent economist who has acted as an adviser to the Bank of England). You will be in contact with the speaker well before the event, so you can check with him or her exactly what the topic for the meeting will be, not least because you will need this for publicity. It's worth asking for an emailed paragraph about what the approach will be so that you have the right words to use both for publicity and for your introduction.

When you have gathered as much up-to-date information as possible, prepare your introduction carefully: you will not escape lightly if you get the speaker's name or title wrong. If you're not sure how to pronounce the name, ask before you start; the speaker won't mind helping you and it's certainly better than making a mistake.

Be positive in your introduction. Presumably you were involved in inviting the speaker to come, so you must think that he or she will be worth hearing. You need to be clear, give the appropriate information firmly and be flattering in your approach. Even if you don't agree with the speaker's views, you can always comment on how fortunate you are to be able to hear such an eminent speaker in person. You can always find good things to say and, while you mustn't sound obsequious, you have a responsibility to both speaker and audience to make them feel glad they have come.

Your responsibilities don't end there. At the end of the talk, there will usually be a question and answer time and you may need to provide the first question to start the session if nobody else seems to be ready to do so. Make a note during the talk of any general question that occurs to you. It isn't your job to be controversial, but you can help the audience by giving them a bit more time to prepare their own questions. You will also need to make notes so that you can thank the speaker at the end. This generally involves picking up two or three of the speaker's main points and saying how fascinating/entertaining/memorable they were, as well as expressing the gratitude of the whole audience. This rounds off the occasion and just as you had to provide a lively and gently flattering start, so you have to conclude in a similar vein, encouraging both speaker and audience to feel that they've thoroughly enjoyed themselves.

Introducing a guest speaker checklist

You've been asked to take the chair for a meeting at which the speaker is a distinguished visitor. Have you:

- ❏ found out as much as you can about the speaker?
- ❏ checked his or her current job title, qualifications and honours, and made sure that you know how to pronounce everything?
- ❏ contacted the speaker (or a secretary) to confirm the exact title of the talk, its subject and how long it will last, and requested information to be used for publicity?
- ❏ prepared your introduction as carefully as you can, with appropriate notes?
- ❏ allowed for a few minutes' talk with the speaker before the session starts to make sure that you are saying the right things?
- ❏ remembered that you must think of one or two questions in case you need them?
- ❏ prepared your words at the end, as far as you can, remembering to speak flatteringly about the talk as you thank the speaker?

Running a meeting

If you're involved in public speaking, the chances are that eventually you will find yourself running a meeting of a committee or society. In this book we're not concerned with the paperwork involved, so you won't find details about preparing agendas or minutes, except as these documents affect or are affected by the way you speak. However, the success or otherwise of a meeting depends a great deal on the skill of the person running it and, as with all aspects of communication, thorough preparation is essential.

Why do you want to chair a meeting? There are good and bad reasons, and it's worth looking briefly at your motives before you agree to do the job. A common reason is that you want to be in control: you enjoy organising other people, whether they want to be organised or not. If you're a good organiser, you may want to be in charge in order to make sure that everything runs smoothly and, in terms of holding a meeting, this might mean that you're unwilling to listen to people who hold up the proceedings by asking awkward questions or disagreeing with what seems to you to be an open and shut case. If you like the feeling of power that being in charge gives you, be wary of chairing a meeting. If you do decide to do so, acknowledge to yourself before you start that you have this controlling tendency and make a conscious effort to listen to others and allow time for discussion, even when you personally can't see the point.

Sometimes, people end up chairing meetings just because nobody else has volunteered. This might seem to be public-spirited, but a meeting that's badly run annoys all who take part and makes them less willing to turn up in future. Don't be too quick to volunteer unless you know that you have the qualities required of a good chairperson.

In the context of student meetings, the person in the chair needs to have at least the qualities we've listed below and preferably also a good voice and a friendly manner:

- the time and dedication to read a great deal of paperwork
- the dedication to prepare thoroughly before every meeting
- willingness to talk to and listen to the people involved in the meeting
- the ability to remain impartial, even in the face of controversy and manipulation
- leadership to impose the rules without offending anyone
- diplomacy to make sure that everyone gets the chance to speak and be listened to.

This is clearly not a task to be undertaken lightly!

One of the first decisions that you, as a new chairperson, have to make is about the type of meeting that will be called (you may find that you chair several different styles of meeting in a short period of time). Some meetings are entirely or primarily about giving and receiving information: you may have a speaker who tells you the background to a topic that you're going to discuss in the future, or you might need some guidance about a topical issue. The meeting is called to hear a presentation and ask questions, but there may be very little actual discussion. Such meetings are unusual but you need to identify one if it happens and alert the people attending to the fact that you don't intend to widen the discussion at that stage.

More commonly, meetings are called to discuss a single issue; it will be introduced and then there will be an opportunity for everyone to ask questions or give an opinion. Again, the people attending the meeting need to know that it will be restricted to the one topic and they won't be expected to try to introduce a different subject. This might require tact on the part of the chairperson, although the situation is made much easier if everyone knows in advance.

The most frequent kind of meeting, however, has an agenda which is a list of subjects for discussion. Committee members will receive this in advance and so can prepare what they want to say. There should be rules about 'any other business' (AOB) at the end of the meeting: generally, any topics to be introduced at that stage should have been notified to the secretary in advance, and the timescale for doing so will probably be laid down. One of the duties of the chairperson is to enforce this rule unless there is a good reason for not doing so. It's sensible to take a reasonable view of this and be willing to allow an additional discussion if it really is both urgent and important.

We've mentioned the different types of meeting because it's the responsibility of the person in the chair to identify which is going to be called and to let people know in advance. People come to meetings with their own agendas, feeling annoyed, frustrated or just longing to talk about a development they really approve of. If they find out at the last minute that the meeting won't allow them to say what's on their minds, they can be cross and, at worst, disruptive.

A good chairperson knows his or her members and is aware of their likely reactions to the items on the agenda. This is difficult at first and it's wise to take advice from the secretary, the previous chairperson or anyone else who will be both helpful and discreet. Part of your preparation is to talk, either face to face or by email, to some of the people who will be coming and find out if they want to speak and, if so, how strong their feelings are. You can then tell if there is likely to be a confrontation and can plan how to handle it.

In such a case, it's important that both sides should be allowed to say what they feel without interruption. If it seems sensible, allocate, say, three minutes to each to introduce their point of view and then ask other committee members for their reactions, as far as possible again making sure that both sides are represented. Two of the most common complaints at meetings are that individuals didn't get the chance to have their say, and that the chairperson appeared to have taken one side or the other from the start. You must be impartial throughout the discussion, even if in the end you need to make a decision. People will respect your position more readily if they can see that both points of view were thoroughly aired.

Meetings can get out of control . . .

The cartoon above shows what can happen if the chairperson doesn't keep control. People will be fed up or angry about what's happening or will simply move away from the group and start their own conversations. It's unlikely that any proper discussion will take place and even less likely that good decisions will be made.

Good preparation means taking the time to plan the agenda carefully, identifying which items are likely to take time, generating discussion and perhaps disagreement, and which items which will probably be agreed within a minute or two. Think, too, of the relative importance of the different topics to be discussed and decide whether to put an 'easy' item first to make everyone relax or whether to tackle a major subject while everyone's fresh and attentive. Avoid putting an item which will probably generate a great deal of discussion too late in the agenda when people are too tired to want to discuss it properly and, as a result, more ready to argue. Timed agendas are usually helpful: you decide the time at which the meeting will finish and say so on the agenda, and then, for your benefit, make a note of the expected length of discussion for each item. Of course you need to be flexible about the detailed timing, but be firm about the time to end, or people will assume that it doesn't mean anything. If there's a major item left and time is running out, defer discussion until the following meeting.

Meeting preparation checklist

You are going to chair a committee meeting in a few days' time. Have you:

- ❏ identified the type of meeting and thought about the implications of this?
- ❏ prepared the agenda, checking the order in which items will be discussed and making your own notes?
- ❏ considered the timing of the whole meeting and individual items?
- ❏ checked that the secretary agrees with your assessment and will send out the agenda in good time?
- ❏ read the relevant papers and the minutes of the previous meeting?
- ❏ talked to some of the people attending the meeting and found out whether they want to speak and how they feel about the issues?

During the meeting, you are responsible for its good order and smooth running. It will help if you start in a friendly and firm way: thank everyone for coming, introduce any new members of the committee, remind members of the main reason for calling the meeting and any time constraints and make a bright, positive start. If people like to have a chat before getting down to business, encourage them to do so before the time at which the meeting starts and then courteously but firmly make sure that you start on time. Try to maintain this tone throughout and praise members whenever you can. A chairperson who smiles and says, 'We got through that really quickly but I think we've been thorough. Thank you, everyone' will encourage people to be quick and thorough in future.

Good order means that you will take the committee through the agenda stage by stage, explaining details if it's necessary, inviting members to speak and recapping from time to time. These are very important stages: if you are in the chair, people must address all their remarks to you and it's up to you to see that they do. Sometimes, students who aren't used to being on a committee get carried away and try to assert themselves over other members, especially when they feel strongly about the issue concerned. If you allow this to happen, the meeting will quickly descend into chaos, with members holding arguments between themselves. Your responsibility is to take action in the pleasantest way possible as soon as you see this is happening and long before a confrontation can develop. Use your voice strongly to call people to order and remind them that they must address the chair. If necessary, stop the discussion for a moment until you are sure that everyone is listening to you. Speak slowly: it's surprising how much attention you will command if you speak clearly and slowly but in a friendly tone of voice.

Recapping the discussion so far, or what has been agreed, is a good way of stopping discussion while you make yourself heard. It's also useful for the secretary who has to record the minutes, as it allows him or her to catch up and helps to ensure that the record is an accurate one. You can get a sense of the meeting, for instance that people feel a discussion has gone on long enough, and you must make sure that all motions are correctly proposed, seconded and agreed. Don't rush this stage, as it's much harder to reopen discussion at a later date if the decision has gone through this procedure and you want to be sure that everyone is happy with the agreement, or at least that everyone has had a chance to put their point of view.

At the same time, you will need to ensure that actions are fairly allocated. Individuals are often required to take action after a meeting and probably on the next occasion to report on what has been done. The secretary will include this request in the minutes, but it's up to you to make sure that the person concerned has heard and agreed. Keeping the pace right is an important aspect of running a meeting: if the discussion and the recording of agreement and action are rushed, members may feel frustrated or bewildered and may want to challenge what appears in the minutes.

You also have the responsibility of making sure that everyone is involved. You might have a quiet, rather shy person who won't put forward an idea unless asked to do so: make sure that he or she is asked at an appropriate moment. On the other hand, you may have someone who tries to take over the meeting, speaking first on every occasion and dominating the discussion. You must restrain such a member firmly but without damping his or her enthusiasm. Always be courteous and insist that everyone else is, too.

Irrelevance is a regular problem for anyone who chairs a meeting. There's usually someone who digresses and, unless checked, starts a subsidiary discussion. This wastes time and energy and makes it harder for you to get through the agenda in time. A smile and a quiet but clear 'Please can we all come back to the subject?' will usually be sufficient. If you have a persistent offender, have a word after the meeting and point out that you want to get through the agenda in a businesslike way and are being held up by irrelevant discussions.

You will have to close the meeting and do so decisively so that you keep to time. Thank the members for their time and their contributions and, if possible, make a positive comment about the discussions, how much they achieved and how pleasant it was that everyone was so helpful. You want them to feel good as they leave, not least because you will be more likely to get their cooperation in the future. If you have the reputation of being an efficient chairperson, you will find that people turn up regularly and actually enjoy the meeting.

Post-meeting checklist

You have just chaired a meeting. It's worth asking yourself the following questions:

- ❏ Did everybody attend (or send their apologies)?
- ❏ Did the meeting keep to time?
- ❏ Do you think that you did enough preparation?
- ❏ Was the atmosphere friendly and cooperative throughout the meeting?
- ❏ Did anyone talk too much and try to dominate?
- ❏ Was anyone very quiet? Did you encourage him or her to contribute?
- ❏ Did you achieve the objectives that you had in mind?
- ❏ What were the best and worst aspects of the meeting?
- ❏ Could you have prevented the worst? Are you pleased with the way you handled it?
- ❏ Is there anything you will do differently next time?

● Public meetings

At the annual general meeting (AGM) of a society, there may be a great many members present and you will have to plan carefully how you are going to chair the session. There are, of course, many ways in which this will be the same as chairing your committee, but there are differences: you will need to project your voice (and your personality); you will have to be firm about asking people to speak, and ready to ask others to wait while everyone listens.

Act at once if you are aware of a breakaway group holding its own meeting: usually a moment of silence during which you simply sit and look at them is enough to make them realise what's happening and rejoin the main meeting. Above all, you must keep order and, to do so effectively, you need friends in key places in the room who will help to reinforce your authority if necessary.

The room in which you're meeting must be a large one to accommodate the numbers, so it's essential that you can be heard. Reread Chapter 2 on speaking to an audience and check that your voice will carry clearly. Try it out beforehand but remember that all those people will absorb sound and you will therefore have to project your voice more and speak more slowly at the meeting itself. Keep the momentum: if you hesitate or appear indecisive, the audience will try to take over. Above all, you have to remain calm and in command: if things get really out of control, stop the meeting until order is restored.

Insist that questions come one at a time, but take them from different parts of the room so that no area of the audience feels neglected. Take your time when answering: if you make a quick decision and it proves to be a bad one, or if you speak crossly to a member of the audience, everybody will have heard what you said. Be ready to ask the secretary to make a note of the question and say that you will need to discuss the issue before coming to a decision but you will circulate your response by email. Always be courteous to questioners, however infuriating they may be.

The key to running any meeting well, whether it's a small committee meeting or the AGM of a large society, is to prepare well. If you've thought carefully about every stage of the occasion, talked and listened to other people and planned a strategy for dealing with the problems you think you might face, you will probably find that everything goes smoothly: if it doesn't, you will have the confidence to handle the situation in a profes-sional way.

Public meeting checklist

If you have to chair a meeting which many people will attend, go through the stages of preparation that we suggested above (pp. 108, 111, 113) for every meeting. In addition:

- ❏ Check that you can be heard in a large room full of people.
- ❏ Be sure of the rules and apply them firmly but courteously.
- ❏ Have a copy of the constitution to hand in case there's a query about procedure.
- ❏ Feel confident that you will be in control. Stop the meeting if you have to, but stay calm and good-tempered in all circumstances.

Top Tips

- • Take a clear, impartial look at whether you should stand for office
- • Speak to a previous holder of the position you're standing for
- • Assess your support and who will campaign for you
- • Remain calm and good-humoured whatever the provocation
- • Smile, make eye contact, and don't fidget in an interview
- • At a meeting, speak slowly and courteously and admit if you're wrong
- • Find out about the speaker you will be introducing and check details with him/her
- • If you're chairing a meeting, enforce the rules in a firm but friendly way
- • A timed agenda helps to keep the meeting under control and stops rambling
- • From time to time recap the discussion/decisions taken, and allocate actions fairly
- • Take soundings before a meeting to find if people feel strongly about an issue
- • At a public meeting, assert your authority firmly but courteously

8 Job Searches and Job Interviews

This chapter helps you to

▶ job search by phone and internet
▶ prepare thoroughly before you make contact
▶ use a careers fair to your advantage
▶ handle a telephone interview effectively
▶ check your Facebook and take care what you reveal
▶ be impressive at your first interview
▶ do it again at your second interview
▶ make an effective interview presentation
▶ wow them on the critical day!

You are now thinking about how to manage your career, and looking for the best way to approach the job market. You will already have contacted your careers office and talked to them about your interests and abilities, reviewing your PDP file in the light of possible careers, and you've probably drafted your CV already and discussed it with the expert staff there. Applying for jobs is a task beyond the scope of this book, but we've given help with both application forms and CVs in *Effective Communication for Arts and Humanities Students* and *Effective Communication for Science and Technology* (see Further Reading). In this chapter, however, we'll be looking at specific aspects of your job search and interview technique.

● Using the telephone for a job search

You know the type of career you'd like to follow, so you carefully read adverts in local and national newspapers and the professional journals which specialise in your chosen area of work. You will respond to any such advert that seems appropriate, but you can also be more proactive in your search and make a direct approach to a company which interests you. If you notice that an organisation has placed a series of adverts for a wide range of posts, you can assume that it's having a recruiting drive and possibly needs more staff than it's currently advertising for. If there is a company you'd really like to work for but you haven't seen a recent advert, check with your careers office to see if it has any useful information (such as the company has been taken over and is advertising under a new name) and try a direct approach.

This sounds like a rash step to take, but the company can always say that it isn't recruiting at the moment, and you've nothing to lose – it probably won't even have your name. You may, on the other hand, find that it has vacancies which haven't yet been advertised, or it may be part of the 'hidden job market', recruiting by word of mouth or only in a particular locality. If this happens, you have put yourself at the head of the queue and may get yourself an interview before anybody else even hears of the job.

Preparation

The key to a successful approach, as usual, is thorough preparation. First, find out as much as you can about the organisations you want to target. You'll see that we said 'organisations' in the plural: there's rarely only one company working in your field, and you don't want to waste all your planning by failing to target several. In any case, you will improve with practice, and it might be worth trying your skills first on a company that you're only mildly interested in, saving the organisation of your dreams until you feel more confident about using the telephone in this way.

There are various ways in which you can get useful information. The company website is an obvious starting place: ask your careers office if they have any brochures from the organisation (or ring reception and ask to be sent a company brochure). Keep an eye on the business and financial sections of a reputable daily paper and acquire a copy of a local paper in the town or city in which the company has its headquarters. Don't rush this stage; it's important that you build up as full a picture as possible of what the organisation does and how it operates.

When you feel ready, prepare yourself a script. You will greet the person who answers the telephone, give your name, subject and university or college, explain that you are interested in working for the organisation and ask if there are any vacancies. You might be put through to the human resources (HR) department, who are the people you really want to speak to, but if not, you can ask for the name of the person you need to speak to, thank your contact and ring off. You will have gained useful information and next time you will have a name to use.

If you make contact with the HR staff, you will need to introduce yourself once more and ask about vacancies. Ask about the company, explaining your area of interest. You might enquire where they usually advertise, if they have a graduate training scheme, when they recruit for it and what they would expect from an applicant. If the replies sound encouraging, you can ask if you might come to speak to someone about career opportunities, or if you could send your CV so that they would have it on file.

Prepare this as an outline script that you can follow if it seems sensible, leaving spaces for the notes you will make at the time, but be ready to abandon your prepared material if you find yourself answering their questions. Always have a copy of your CV in front of you so that if your enquiry turns into a mini-interview, you have something to refer to.

Self-preparation

As this might happen at any point, make sure that your self-preparation is also thorough. Before you pick up the telephone, make sure that you have plenty of time (you don't know how long any call might take) and that you won't have any interruptions at your end. Have paper and pen for notes, and your CV and any other useful material within easy reach. Sit on a comfortable but upright chair to give yourself maximum back support and try to look as businesslike as possible. Imagine that your contact can see you and is assessing you for the job you want. This has the effect of making you more alert and your response more formal (contrast this with the way in which you might sit to chat to a friend – lounging, perhaps having a drink, putting your feet up).

Think positively. Even if the company doesn't have any vacancies at present, suggest sending a CV that can be filed for the future. Don't allow yourself to be discouraged, as this will show in your voice. You might suggest doing some vacation work for it, even without pay. Recently, a new graduate who wanted to break into television research for a particular subject (a very difficult aspiration, as the work is always oversubscribed) rang a well-respected researcher to ask him some questions for her dissertation. Later, when she rang back to thank him and said how much she would like to work in that area, he suggested that she might carry out a specific piece of research for him, just for expenses. She did it well, knowing that the chance to quote experience and perhaps even have her name associated with the programme were, at that stage, more valuable than salary. Be positive, and listen carefully for any lead that could be helpful in the future.

The telephone cold call is a two-way process: you are finding out about the company just as much as it is finding out about you. Notice the response you get: if it seems friendly and helpful, you are encouraged to think of the organisation as having a good atmosphere; if the person on the line is discourteous, abrupt or offhand, perhaps the whole company is the same. This is unlikely to be true, but the telephone receptionist is an ambassador for his or her company, and we all judge a great deal by first impressions.

It takes courage to use the telephone in your search for employment, but it can be rewarding. Work through your list of organisations and you'll feel increasingly confident as you proceed. It's a good idea, nevertheless, to dial

141 before the number, so that your call can't be traced and if you stumble or get embarrassed as soon as you start, you can put the phone down and they will never know who rang, leaving you free to try again when you've had more practice!

Telephone job search checklist

You are planning to contact a list of organisations in the hope that one of them might offer you a job interview. Have you:

- ❏ listed the organisations, starting with one that you don't particularly favour?
- ❏ found out enough about each organisation to ask sensible questions?
- ❏ prepared a script which you might follow if it seems appropriate?
- ❏ thought about the questions you would like to ask?
- ❏ planned your time so that you won't be rushed?
- ❏ made sure that you won't be interrupted?
- ❏ put paper, pen and your CV within reach?
- ❏ considered where and how you will sit and taken a deep breath to help you to relax?

● Careers fairs

Towards the end of your course, your careers office will probably encourage you to attend one or more careers fairs on university or college premises. These provide an excellent opportunity for companies to meet and assess likely young graduates who might be interested in becoming their employees, perhaps joining a graduate training scheme. At the same time, such fairs are useful for you, allowing you to see something of the range of organisations offering employment and to meet and talk to some of their staff.

There's a potential problem in that you're on your own premises; you might have come from a class or a students' union meeting, and it's difficult to feel as if you're actually going to a job interview. This feeling is increased by the welcome you'll receive, which is likely to be more in terms of 'let's have a chat' than a formal invitation. Nevertheless, this might be the equivalent of a first interview and the way you react might determine whether the contact goes any further. Make sure that you look at least tidy and enthusiastic; if you're too casual, your interviewer might think that you really aren't bothered whether or not you work for his or her company.

At this stage, you're more likely to meet HR staff than experts in the field and they will probably ask you general questions about your course, what you like and dislike, what your other interests are and why you're interested in one of the careers they offer. These seem simple questions, but beware of the offhand comment, any suggestion of superiority or saying more than you would have done if you'd been on your guard. Start off by being formal and become more relaxed only if the interviewer does so first. Always think carefully about the implications of the questions and your answers. Listen to what the interviewer says and the way in which he or she responds to you; you are judging the company quite as much as they are judging you.

Careers fair checklist

You are going to a careers fair later today. Remember the preparation suggested below:

- ❑ Have you checked the time and place of the fair and made sure that you won't be short of time if you want to speak to people?
- ❑ Are you reasonably well presented and tidy?
- ❑ Have you a couple of copies of your CV to give to useful contacts?
- ❑ Have you a notebook available to record any helpful information such as your impressions of a company, or contact names?
- ❑ Have you made a note of companies you'd like to talk to and questions you want to ask?

There's an overlap between the careers fair interview and the first interview proper, and nowadays this latter may be by telephone rather than face to face.

● Telephone interviews

Increasingly, companies are holding preliminary interviews by telephone and you (and the people you share accommodation with) need to be aware of this and ready to respond in an appropriate manner. The date and time of the call are usually prearranged, but this can't be guaranteed and it's most important that everyone is ready to answer the telephone courteously and take a message if necessary. If you are the applicant, you need to keep a copy of your CV and a notepad within easy reach so that you can be prepared for an interview at short notice.

Most of the advice we gave in discussing the telephone job-search applies equally to telephone interviews: prepare questions you'd like to ask, answers you're likely to give (especially the 'Why are you interested in this job/career?' kind), be formal and courteous and don't rush your answers. As the interviewer can't see you, it's wise to say 'May I think about that for a moment, please?', rather than allowing a long silence on the line. Check the interviewer's name at the start, asking for it to be spelt if necessary; you might subsequently need to write to this person and this is the best opportunity to make sure that you've recorded the name correctly. Don't talk too much: remember that it's possible to talk yourself out of as well as into a job. You can always give a short answer and let the interviewer ask a further question if he or she wants to, which is usually better than getting carried away – telephone calls are expensive, the whole session will probably last no more than about fifteen minutes and the interviewer won't want to listen to your life story for long. Don't interrupt the questioner, even if you think that you can guess what the question is going to be; let the interviewer guide the way in which the interview proceeds.

Your tone of voice is enormously important in a telephone conversation. You can't see each other, so both speakers have to pick up on each other's attitude and emotion by listening to the tone that is used. You want to give an impression of professionalism, intelligence and enthusiasm, and it's possible to do this by the way you speak. We said earlier that sitting in an upright, alert way is a good start; make sure that you feel bright and positive throughout the call, and as the interview finishes, smile and thank the interviewer. He or she can't see the smile but it can be heard in your voice, which will leave a lasting good impression.

30-minute telephone interview checklist

You have been told to expect a first interview by telephone in half an hour's time. Go through the following checklist:

- ❑ Have you made sure that the telephone will be free for you to answer it?
- ❑ Are you sure that you won't be interrupted?
- ❑ Do you know where you'll sit and where you'll put your notes?
- ❑ Are pen and paper within reach for making notes during the interview?
- ❑ Have you found and looked through a copy of your CV?
- ❑ Have you thought about why you're interested in this career and this job?
- ❑ Will you be able to ask a few useful and relevant questions?

● Facebook checking

You might naturally assume that your first interview is just that: the first time that you and your prospective employer have the chance to meet and assess one another. Not necessarily. Nowadays, companies are likely to have checked you out first, using a social networking site such as Facebook. They will be trying to find out if you look worth interviewing, or looking for guidance as to the type of questions they might ask you when you do meet.

This isn't an altogether welcome development, but you need to take it into account. When you produced your wall on Facebook, you probably assumed only one audience, your family and friends. To you, it probably doesn't even feel like a public space, but of course it is. Although a potential employer will have only limited access to your information, it may be enough to form a lasting impression.

You might, reasonably, feel that you want an employer to hire the 'real you' and so you don't care what they see about you on Facebook, but are you sure that your wall does represent you as you really are, or is it just a jokey version? An employer might ignore 'Jedi' as a response to a question about religion, or 'the opposite sex' as a description of your interests – such responses are common – but if, in a moment of weakness, you have revealed more about yourself than you would want an employer to see, you might want to make changes before you start job hunting.

Recent research suggests that employers are most influenced by photographs: your family and friends may love the picture of you pole dancing in Ibiza, for instance, but an employer who expects you to deal soberly and diplomatically with the public might have some doubts. Equally, if you might be asked to join a dynamic team and all the pictures on your site are of you standing alone on a windswept mountain, you might be giving the impression that you are not a keen team player.

Some people decide to 'clean up' their wall before job hunting, just as they might put a special ringtone on their mobile phone to alert them to incoming calls from employers, or create a new email account which has a less jovial address; others even temporarily alter their name on Facebook, slightly misspelling their surname, for example, so that access is limited to those who are in the know. These are options you might want to consider; on the other hand, you may feel that your site gives the perfect picture of you and your interests and decide to leave it as it stands. It's your choice, but do give it some thought.

First interview

Your first interview might take place at a careers fair or by telephone, or you may instead be called to company premises on a date and at a time that have been given you. Do you know how to get there and how long the journey is likely to take? You may have been sent a map, but if not, you can download one from the internet by using the organisation's postcode, and then, if the journey looks complicated, you could ring and ask the receptionist for local details. It's essential that you arrive at the best possible time: not so early that you have to sit for an hour becoming increasingly nervous but certainly not at the last minute so that you have no time to sit and calm down. If you can, check out the journey in advance, remembering that a car or taxi is likely to take longer in the rush hour.

Once you've done this, record the date, time and address and how to get there in your diary or somewhere else so that you can't possibly mislay it. Failure to turn up correctly means that you've lost the job before you've even started the interview process. Now you can start the real preparation for your interview.

Preparation

Your first call should be the careers office, for two reasons: the staff might have up-to-date information about the company you are going to, and they may give you a practice interview so that you hear the sort of questions you might be asked and have the chance to go through your answers with expert advice. Careers staff aren't, of course, likely to be experts in the particular area of work you've chosen, but the first interview will probably be run by a panel of HR personnel who will ask general questions. Detailed technical or scientific questions, for example, would arise at the second stage. Any information that you can obtain about 'your' company will be valuable in showing your interest in and awareness of current conditions in the industry, so look again at its website and keep an eye on the national press in case there's a report or a comment that might be useful to you – again, the careers staff may be able to help.

This is also the time to go back to your CV or the copy of your application form. Remind yourself of what you said, and look for possible areas of questioning. In the first interview, you'll probably be asked about your work experience, especially if you're a mature student, and about your attitudes to work: do you enjoy teamwork, how do you feel about risk taking or decision making, what aspects of your course have you enjoyed or disliked and why? How good are you at planning your time? Do you like taking responsibility? Can you communicate complex ideas to a general audience? If you think back over the past two or three years, you may find that you've had more experience of these challenges than seemed possible at first. Teamwork might have come through a group project or taking part in a play; you might enjoy a sport that involves a certain amount of risk; you might have made decisions in preparing a project or planning a summer event in your hall; you might have been treasurer of a society and had to take financial responsibility; you had to plan your dissertation timetable; you might have had experience through a vacation job of communicating your work to outsiders. It's not likely that you've done all these things, but other people will be in the same position. Go through your work, leisure activities and vacation jobs, and make notes of all the experiences you've had that could be useful in answering such questions.

Appropriate dress

Decide what you will wear for your interview. It's worth remembering that the interviewer will look at you before you speak and first impressions can be critical. What you choose will depend to some extent on your area of work, but it's best to be smart and formal. A suit and quietly coloured shirt is usually appropriate, with a pair of sensible, smart shoes. Avoid anything fussy or brightly coloured; large pieces of jewellery are distracting, as is a loudly patterned tie. It's unwise to wear anything new for the occasion: it might prove awkward in some way or uncomfortable, and neither you nor the interviewer wants to be distracted from the interview itself. Think about appropriate NVC, especially at the beginning of the interview (see below). Discuss all these details with friends and listen to their interview experiences. If you're unsure about any aspect, ask your tutor or the careers staff. It takes time and effort to prepare for an interview, but you will be very glad that you were so thorough.

First impressions

When you arrive for your interview, give your name, the main interviewer's name and the time of the interview to the receptionist, who will probably ask you to sit and wait. This isn't easy, as you're feeling nervous and your rivals may be sitting around you. Remember the advice we gave about controlling nerves before a presentation; it's just the same: relax your shoulders, take a deep breath and release it slowly. Look for a company magazine (there are usually some around in a reception area) and skim it to see if there are any articles or comments of interest to you and the work you're hoping to do. Smile at the competition and greet them briefly, but try not to get involved in conversation: almost inevitably, you will feel that they're better qualified or experienced than you are, whether this is true or not.

When you're called for interview, walk in briskly with your head up, smile and greet your interviewer or panel, be ready to shake hands if they offer to do so and wait to be asked to sit down. The interviewers will introduce themselves and you can smile at each as they do so. The interview will then begin. It's likely that the first one or two questions will be straightforward: did you have difficulty finding the building, have you visited the town before and similar innocuous topics, designed to help you to feel at ease. Answer politely but briefly. This part of the interview isn't as meaningless as it might seem: the panel is noticing that you're nervous (rightly) but that you're in control; you appear confident but not too much so; you are making eye contact and looking alert and willing to communicate; you appear friendly and genuinely interested. These are important signals for the interviewers in assessing how good a colleague you will make.

Answering questions

The questions will soon become more challenging and this is where all your preparation will be so helpful. You might be asked about aspects of your course, your leisure activities, your work experience; you may be faced with more personal questions about your interest in the career and why you think you are suited to it; you may be asked about your strengths and weaknesses (be as honest as you can, but it helps if you've thought about these in advance); your ambitions ('What would you like to be doing in five years' time?' is a favoured question) and your management qualities. Keep your answers brief and to the point, and make eye contact with each questioner in turn. As we've said before, it's good to take your time, especially with a difficult question: the pause helps you to assess not only what you want to say, but also how you will say it. If you don't understand a question, ask for it to be repeated or clarified, and be ready to say if you don't know the answer.

Concluding the interview

Towards the end of the interview, you'll be asked if you have any questions. You need to have prepared two or three: training is always a sensible topic to ask about, or the variety of work experience. Never ask about money or holidays! If all your questions have already been answered, say so with a smile and thank the interviewers.

An interview is never over until the door has closed behind you. When you are told you can go, you'll again smile and say thank you, and walk briskly to the door. Don't assume that you will hear no more from the interviewers; sometimes you will be called back before you leave the room ('Oh, we forgot to ask . . .') and there will be another question. This can be deliberate, to see how you respond to the sudden extra stress or whether you answer carelessly because your guard is down. Answer calmly and pause to make sure that you really can go and then, as the door closes behind you, it really is time to relax – although not too much until you're actually off the premises.

First-interview checklist

You will be going in a few days' time to the first interview for a job you would seriously like to get. Have you:

❏ found out how to get there and how long the journey is likely to take?
❏ checked the company website and your careers office for up-to-date information?
❏ looked at your CV or application form and thought of questions you might be asked?
❏ thought about your course and your particular interests (and dislikes)?
❏ considered sensibly what you have to offer this job, and what you would like to see it offer you, for instance in terms of training?
❏ analysed your own ambitions and what you would like to achieve?
❏ planned a few questions that you would like to ask?
❏ decided what you will wear?
❏ had a practice interview with your careers office?

● Second interview

You've been through the ordeal of a first interview, but the business of getting the job you want isn't over yet. You've been invited to go for a further interview, probably but not certainly at the same place you went to for the first. You have the advantage of knowing how to get there and how long it will take, and you also have the great benefit of knowing that the organisation is seriously interested in you. Nobody is going to ask you back unless they feel that there's a good chance they'll want to employ you.

However, this interview is likely to be more testing than the first. The panel will probably consist of experts in your area of work, possibly including the manager for whom you would be working if you were appointed. The organisation liked the sound of you at your first interview and now wants to make sure that you are the most suitable person available in terms of your knowledge and willingness to learn and your personality as a member of the group. Don't, incidentally, underestimate the 'people chemistry' aspect. You might be a budding Einstein, but if they feel that you might be irritable, difficult to work with or unreliable, they are more likely to choose the second best brain with the more pleasing personality. After all, you can always be trained and gaps in your knowledge can be filled, but if you antagonise everyone around you, the company will soon regret the appointment. Be as courteous and as friendly (within the limits of an interview!) as you reasonably can.

Preparing once again

You will need to go through all the stages of preparation again: talking to the careers office, looking at the company website to see if there have been any changes and, especially this time, making sure that your professional knowledge is as accurate and up to date as possible. Read a good daily newspaper in case there's been some new legislation or company report which you might be able to refer to during the interview: it's always impressive when the candidate does this, and it might make you different from everyone else they're seeing that day. Think again about your course and the decisions you made: why did you take those particular options and do they relate to the work you hope to do? Think of any implications of your work that might be topical, such as environmental or safety issues. Can you think of any connections between your final-year project and the organisation's work, and any further research that might be interesting? What would you like to do if the opportunity occurred, for instance, to learn another language or work abroad for a year or two? The more you consider these and similar topics, the better prepared you will be and the less likely it is that you will be taken aback or unable to answer questions at the interview. You will, of course, make plans about what you will wear and what time you will leave for your interview just as you did for the first one, but this time you might be going for a whole day or even longer. Accommodation will probably have been arranged for you, but if you haven't heard, check: you might need a recommendation from the company about where to stay, if you don't know the area.

A long interview session will be divided into various activities. You might have to take a psychometric test to see how suited you are to the career you've chosen or you might have to take part in some kind of group activity, such as a business game. Discuss the possibilities with your careers office, and, if possible, get some practice. At some stage, you will also have to give a presentation.

Making an interview presentation

You will very probably have been asked to make a presentation at this interview, and the earlier parts of this book will be useful, especially Chapter 2 and the section of Chapter 4 which deals with notes. Think back to any presentations you gave as part of your course and reread any handouts on presentation techniques that you were given. Then look carefully at the guidance you were given about the subject on which you have to speak.

Handling a set topic You may, although it's unlikely, simply be given a subject to talk about. If this happens, it will almost certainly be a wide topic and you will have to do the same narrowing-down exercise that we mentioned earlier in the context of group presentations (see pp. 90–1). You might be able to choose your own topic within the framework set; for instance, we heard of an occasion on which the candidate was asked to speak about any contemporary figure who interested him (he chose Bill Gates, and got the job!). If you're given a subject that you don't know much about, don't panic: the chances are that nobody else will be any better informed, you have time to do some research and you can't say much in the ten minutes or so that's the usual time allocation.

Choosing a topic It's much more probable that you'll be given a certain amount of choice, the likely suggestions being 'anything to do with the area of work you're interested in' or, where it's appropriate, 'any scientific or technical subject that interests you' or, less helpfully, 'anything you like'. If the subject area is specified, you now have the task of deciding exactly what aspect you will choose.

There are various possibilities. If you have to speak about the work you're applying to do, then you have the disadvantage that the people listening will certainly know more than you do, but the advantage that you can speak with genuine enthusiasm, which is always a good selling point. Have you had a part-time or vacation job which is relevant? Research the subject, using your careers office, the internet, any lecturers whose subject is useful in this context, magazines, newspapers, and so on. Try to find an unusual angle that might appeal to your audience, and, if you can, mention a recent or topical development. If they have to listen to several presentations about their own area of work, they could get bored, and someone who has thought of a different approach would stand out.

You might choose to speak about some aspect of your study, such as your final-year project. The disadvantages are that you may be bored with it by now and that originally it was perhaps shared with someone else. You will need to rethink it and, almost certainly, choose one small part of the original project. Is it possible to follow up on your topic, looking at an aspect which you didn't have time to cover before? This might be more exciting but it could involve you in a great deal of work in a short time. Is there another part of your course which you found especially interesting and would enjoy looking at again? Have you used your knowledge in a vacation job? This would have the bonus that you would be speaking about work in a commercial or industrial setting, which would appeal to your audience. If you do this, be sure to ask permission from the company concerned, so that it can warn you if any of your information is commercially sensitive. The best solution, if it's possible, is to speak about a leisure interest which is relevant to the position you've applied for, but which you can discuss with a sense of personal involvement and enthusiasm. Don't, of course, pretend to have an interest which isn't genuine: you could easily be caught out by the superior knowledge of one of the panel.

It's more daunting to be told that you have a completely free choice of subject. Where on earth do you begin? You could talk about some aspect of your study, but it might seem limited, as if you had no other interest. You could talk about one of your leisure activities, as long as it's unusual; you don't want to risk finding that an earlier candidate has spoken about the same thing. There are two major criteria: the aspect you talk about must be small enough, or capable of being subdivided, for you to say something interesting in about ten minutes, and you must be genuinely enthusiastic about it, so that your face lights up, your voice is bright and you make your audience feel as excited about the subject as you do. If you can do this, the subject itself doesn't matter very much; it's your commitment that convinces your listeners.

Preparing your talk   Having chosen your topic, you must prepare it in the ways we've discussed earlier (see especially Chapters 2 and 4). The timing (see pp. 79–81) is critical. If you've been given ten minutes, rehearse until your talk is exactly eight minutes so that there's the little bit of spare time that can make all the difference. This is an occasion when to overrun is potentially disastrous: your interviewers want to see how good a manager you are, whether they might want you to represent the company at some time, how conscientiously you will use their resources. They are also very busy and another candidate is waiting; if you take too long, you've disturbed their schedules and they won't be pleased. So practise your talk several times, with your visual aids if you are going to use any.

Visual aids in an interview   The question of visual aids is a difficult one. You may not know what is possible in the room, for example whether there is the right equipment, if there are blinds, and so on. You've also got limited time. Think of all that can go wrong with a data projector, especially if you're using an unfamiliar laptop, and how long it can take to boot up, and you might rule it out unless you've specifically been told to use it. A flipchart is very informal and it isn't easy to draw or write in front of people when you're nervous. The OHP is a possible choice, but you must be sure that one is available. Ring the company and ask. If they are happy for you to use an

OHP, prepare your material on the computer, taking care with colour and font size, and using only a small number of slides: three or four are plenty for ten minutes. Don't take too long to prepare them, to the detriment of the rest of your preparation. They need to be good quality, but you need as much time as possible for what you are going to say.

You might consider that such a short talk can be given without any visual aids, and you could be right, but think about the subject and make sure that, if you dismiss the idea of visual material, your talk will still be clear and easy to follow and interesting to listen to. If you feel that just one picture will help, take several hard copies with you so that you can give one to each member of the panel and still have one to talk from. Whether you use visual aids or not, rehearse your talk in a formal way, standing up and using notes, so that you feel comfortable with it when you get to your interview.

Giving your talk Remember all the advice you've been given about taking your time, breathing deeply, relaxing your shoulders and being ready to pause before attempting an answer to a difficult question. All these techniques will now help you; as long as you speak slowly and clearly, keep to time and are obviously interested in what you're saying, you will do well. It's a short presentation, and your interviewers will want to see how you cope rather than criticise what you say. Smile at them as you start and as you finish and be as confident as you can (even though you're also nervous!).

The interview day

During your interview day, or perhaps even the night before, you will probably have to have a meal with the other candidates. You'll be told, no doubt, that this isn't part of the interview procedure and you can relax. Don't believe a word of it. Of course you'll be assessed in an informal way, as your potential employers will want to know how you mix with other people, how you can relate to strangers and how you cope with what is, inevitably, a stressful situation. It's just as bad for everyone else as it is for you, which is a comforting thought. Be courteous and friendly but watch what you say. Don't be tempted to unnerve competitors for the job or undermine their confidence. They may be colleagues in the future and they won't forget! Ask 'innocent' questions, about where they live and what their interests are, and listen more than you talk. Don't drink too much and never be critical of the organisation you hope to work for or the planning of the day.

The interview itself

Eventually, you will get to the interview itself. Relax as far as you can, breathe well and smile as you greet the panel. When you're asked to sit down, do so, sitting well back in the chair so that you have maximum back support; you should be sitting in an upright, alert way, looking both comfortable and professional. As before, the first one or two questions are likely to be general, but they will soon become more testing and your reactions will be important, more so in some ways than the answers you give. Don't be afraid to say if you don't know, and take your time over difficult 'What would you do if ...?' questions. If you feel that you've given a weak answer, think quickly about whether you can improve it by starting again; if you can't, forget it. It's a problem that everyone faces at interview. Keep your answers short but, if it seems appropriate, be ready to add 'I could say more about that if you'd like me to.' Listen carefully to the questions and don't interrupt the questioner; you need to give an impression of confidence and taking your time is a good indicator of this.

Pausing also helps you to feel in control of the situation. Never become aggressive, even if you feel that the questioning has become unfair; it might have been designed precisely to see how you react under pressure. Don't be flippant or make remarks which seem humorous at the time but which you might regret later. Make eye contact with each questioner in turn and be ready to smile.

If you are a mature student, you are likely to be asked about your previous work experience, and you will have thought about this in advance. Don't go into great length about it, but summarise the aspects which are relevant to the job in prospect. You are more likely than a new graduate to be asked about a starting salary, which might be lower than what you've earned in the past. Decide before the interview what is the lowest salary you would be willing to accept and stick to this unless something said at the interview persuades you to change your mind. Be careful not to get carried away and end up accepting too little.

When you're invited to ask questions, do so, using those you have prepared and thanking your panel for their answers. At last the interview is over, but, as before, don't relax too soon, certainly not before you're out of sight of everyone belonging to the company: the door might have closed on the panel but someone else might see you and make a comment; the receptionist will be noticing all the candidates and the way they behave. When you're outside the main door, you can at last relax.

Of course you hope that you've been successful, but if not, ring the company and ask where they thought your weaknesses were. You will get good pointers for the next time and the person you speak to will be impressed by your perseverance and thoroughness. It can also happen that the person who was offered the job turned it down and that when you ring, they are desperately looking for someone else. You never know, you might be lucky. In any case, you've gained good experience and next time you will do even better.

Second interview checklist

You are preparing for the second interview for the job you want. Have you:

- ❏ found out as much up-to-date information about the company as you can?
- ❏ discussed the interview with your careers office?
- ❏ prepared your presentation, with visual aids if you feel that they are needed?
- ❏ made sure that you have timed your presentation exactly?
- ❏ checked what visual aids equipment will be available, if any?
- ❏ reviewed your final project or dissertation and assessed its relevance to the job?
- ❏ considered your work experience and leisure activities for examples you could use?
- ❏ prepared a few questions that you can ask?
- ❏ thought carefully about what you can offer the job and what you would like it to offer you?

The ability to speak well is increasingly important, whatever the subject you've studied or your chosen career. If you believe in your own ability to persuade an audience of your point of view, you are likely to have a successful future. Be nervous, of course, but be confident: it's a winning combination!

Top Tips

- Be proactive – use your careers office, newspapers and the internet to find work
- Prepare thoroughly before making a phone call
- Always have your up-to-date CV nearby to refer to
- Decide what they might ask you and what you want to ask them
- Ensure Facebook doesn't trap you – check what potential employers might see
- Choose your presentation topic with care, prepare and rehearse
- First impressions count – make eye contact and smile
- Listen carefully to questions and take your time in answering
- Keep your answers brief and to the point – don't waffle
- Don't relax until you're outside the building!

Further Reading

Becker, L. (2002) *How to Manage your Arts, Humanities and Social Science Degree.* Basingstoke: Palgrave Macmillan.

Becker, L. (2004) *How to Manage your Distance and Open Learning Course.* Basingstoke: Palgrave Macmillan.

Becker, L. (2004) *How to Manage your Postgraduate Course.* Basingstoke: Palgrave Macmillan.

Becker, L. and Price, D. (2003) *How to Manage your Science and Technology Degree.* Basingstoke: Palgrave Macmillan.

Cottrell, S. (2008) *The Study Skills Handbook,* 3rd edn. Basingstoke: Palgrave Macmillan.

Cottrell, S. (2010) *Skills for Success: The Personal Development Planning Handbook,* 2nd edn. Basingstoke: Palgrave Macmillan.

Fanthome, C. (2004) *Work Placements – A Survival Guide for Students.* Basingstoke: Palgrave Macmillan.

Littleford, D, Halstead, J. And Mulraine, C. (2004) *Career Skills: Opening Doors into the Job Market.* Basingstoke: Palgrave Macmillan.

Peck, J. and Coyle, M. (2005) *The Student's Guide to Writing,* 2nd edn. Basingstoke: Palgrave Macmillan.

van Emden, J. (2001) *Effective Communication for Science and Technology.* Basingstoke: Palgrave Macmillan.

van Emden, J. (2005) *Writing for Engineers,* 3rd edn. Basingstoke: Palgrave Macmillan.

van Emden, J. and Becker, L. (2003) *Effective Communication for Arts and Humanities Students.* Basingstoke: Palgrave Macmillan.

Index